Cooking Light

chill

SMOOTHIES, SLUSHES, SHAKES, JUICES, DRINKS & ICES

southern sweet tea
granita, page 196

Cooking Light

chill

SMOOTHIES, SLUSHES, SHAKES, JUICES, DRINKS & ICES

Oxmoor
House®

ISBN-13: 978-0-8487-3951-5
ISBN-10: 0-8487-3951-5
Library of Congress Control Number: 2013932096

Printed in the United States of America
First Printing 2013

Be sure to check with your health-care provider before making any changes in your diet.

Oxmoor House

Editorial Director: Leah McLaughlin
Creative Director: Felicity Keane
Senior Brand Manager: Michelle Turner Aycock
Senior Editor: Andrea C. Kirkland, M.S., R.D.
Managing Editor: Rebecca Benton

Cooking Light Chill

Editor: Shaun Chavis
Art Director: Claire Cormany
Project Editor: Megan McSwain Yeatts
Assistant Designer: Allison Sperando Potter
Director, Test Kitchen: Elizabeth Tyler Austin
Assistant Directors, Test Kitchen:
    Julie Christopher, Julie Gunter
Recipe Developers and Testers: Wendy Ball, R.D.,
    Victoria E. Cox, Tamara Goldis,
    Stefanie Maloney, Callie Nash, Karen Rankin,
    Leah Van Deren
Recipe Editor: Alyson Moreland Haynes
Food Stylists: Margaret Monroe Dickey,
    Catherine Crowell Steele
Photography Director: Jim Bathie
Senior Photographer: Helene Dujardin
Senior Photo Stylist: Kay E. Clarke
Photo Stylist: Mindi Shapiro Levine
Assistant Photo Stylist: Mary Louise Menendez
Senior Production Manager: Greg A. Amason

Contributors

Project Editor: Katie Strasser
Recipe Developers and Testers: David Bonom,
    Ruth Cousineau, Mary Drennen, Iris O'Brien
Copy Editors: Julie Bosche, Dolores Hydock
Proofreader: Erica Midkiff
Indexer: Mary Ann Laurens
Interns: Megan Branagh, Frances Gunnells,
    Susan Kemp, Sara Lyon, Staley McIlwain,
    Jeffrey Preis, Emily Robinson, Maria Sanders,
    Julia Sayers
Food Stylists: Mary Drennen, Erica Hopper
Photographers: Becky Stayner
Photo Stylists: Mary Clayton Carl, Missie Crawford

Time Home Entertainment Inc.

Publisher: Jim Childs
VP, Strategy & Business Development:
    Steven Sandonato
Executive Director, Marketing Services:
    Carol Pittard
Executive Director, Retail & Special Sales:
    Tom Mifsud
Director, Bookazine Development & Marketing:
    Laura Adam
Executive Publishing Director: Joy Butts
Associate Publishing Director: Megan Pearlman
Finance Director: Glenn Buonocore
Associate General Counsel: Helen Wan

Cooking Light®

Editor: Scott Mowbray
Deputy Editor: Phillip Rhodes
Executive Editor, Food: Ann Taylor Pittman
Special Publications Editor:
    Mary Simpson Creel, MS, RD
Senior Food Editor: Julianna Grimes
Senior Editor: Cindy Hatcher
Associate Food Editor: Timothy Q. Cebula
Assistant Editor, Nutrition: Sidney Fry, MS, RD
Assistant Editors: Kimberly Holland, Phoebe Wu
Test Kitchen Director: Vanessa T. Pruett
Assistant Test Kitchen Director:
    Tiffany Vickers Davis
Recipe Testers and Developers: Robin Bashinsky,
    Adam Hickman, Deb Wise
Art Directors: Fernande Bondarenko,
    Shawna Kalish
Junior Deputy Art Director: Alexander Spacher
Associate Art Director: Rachel Lasserre
Junior Designer: Hagen Stegall
Photo Director: Kristen Schaefer
Assistant Photo Editor: Amy Delaune
Senior Photographer: Randy Mayor
Senior Photo Stylist: Cindy Barr
Photo Stylist: Leigh Ann Ross
Food Styling Assistant: Blakeslee Wright
Chief Food Stylist: Charlotte Autry
Senior Food Stylist: Kellie Gerber Kelley
Copy Chief: Maria Parker Hopkins
Assistant Copy Chief: Susan Roberts
Research Editor: Michelle Gibson Daniels
Editorial Production Director: Liz Rhoades
Production Editor: Hazel R. Eddins
Assistant Production Editor: Josh Rutledge
Administrative Coordinator: Carol D. Johnson
Cookinglight.com Editor: Allison Long Lowery
Nutrition Editor: Holley Johnson Grainger, MS, RD
Production Assistant: Mallory Brasseale

To order additional publications,
call 1-800-765-6400 or 1-800-491-0551.

To search, savor, and share thousands
of recipes, visit myrecipes.com

Front flap: Peanut Butter-Berry Smoothie, pg. 60
Back cover: Orange, Banana, and Pineapple
    Frappé, page 57

welcome

It's time to take drinks to a place of smarter refreshment. In the *Cooking Light* Test Kitchen, we've created cold treats that can quench your thirst, cool you on a hot day, satisfy your sweet tooth with fewer calories, and dose you with nutrients and antioxidants from fruit and vegetables.

Cooking Light Chill **revives the meaning of refreshment**—restoring your energy and supporting your body—with more than **120 recipes designed to be healthier for you.** Inside these pages, you'll find:

- **Nutritious, delicious ideas for your healthy lifestyle.** Treats made with fresh fruits and vegetables give you great flavor plus the good-for-you vitamins and antioxidants you need.

- **Recipes using all-natural sweeteners** to help you feel good about what you're putting in your body and let you control the sugar.

- **Smoothies you can make in minutes** for a quick energy-boosting breakfast, and juices for a post-workout pick-me-up.

- **Creamy shakes, frosty slushes, and fruity ices** (skip the syrups!) for dessert: *Cooking Light Chill* includes lower-calorie, healthier versions of childhood favorites—and some new drinks, too.

- **Recipes designed to be made using everyday kitchen tools:** You won't need a pricey blender or juicer.

- **More than 80 dairy-free versions** give people with dietary restrictions plenty of tummy-pleasing options.

- **Easy, reliable recipes you can count on.** Every recipe is Test Kitchen–approved and meets the same nutrition guidelines used in *Cooking Light* magazine.

To your health!
The Editors of *Cooking Light*

berry and banana
smoothie, page 30

milk chocolate almond
shake, page 100

contents

orange-carrot refresher,
page 138

spicy mango granita,
page 197

juices & drinks......................120
Use your own produce to make refreshing
thirst-quenchers.

ices......................................164
Enjoy a scoop for a light dessert.

the basics

Making cold treats at home lets you use ingredients you feel good about. Master the basics in three simple steps: Get some gear, gather great ingredients, and use smart techniques.

STEP #1:
GET SOME GEAR

You only need a few simple pieces of equipment to make the drinks and ices in this book. (Chances are you already have many of them!)

1. BLENDER
All of the recipes in *Cooking Light Chill* were tested with a standard home blender—you don't need a specialty blender or expensive juicer.

2. GLASSES
Presentation can make any drink more enjoyable. Choose fun glasses for your smoothies, shakes, slushes, and juices.

3. HANDHELD JUICER
This common low-tech bar tool is handy when you need to juice a lot of citrus at once; it keeps the seeds separate from the juice, too.

4. IMMERSION BLENDER
Also known as a handheld blender or stick blender, an immersion blender can save you from washing an extra dish or two: You can blend ingredients in the bowl, glass, or pot you're already using.

5. PITCHERS AND JARS
Chill, serve, and store drinks with style.

6. REAMER
Twist this simple tool inside half of a citrus to extract the fruit's juice quickly.

7. STRAINER OR CHINOIS
Use one of these to strain pulp from juices, especially when one of the ingredients is citrus or pineapple.

8. COUNTERTOP ICE CREAM MAKER
Some ices are made in an ice cream maker. Countertop models can freeze a mix in as little as 20 minutes.

STEP #2:
GATHER GREAT INGREDIENTS

choose your base flavor:

This list of ingredients includes some beverage-making staples, plus a few wild cards to keep things interesting. Many smoothies and shakes call for frozen fruit—see page 19 for instructions on how to freeze your own.

AVOCADOS: Around the world this fruit is used in sweet drinks. Use a soft avocado for best results—an avocado should yield to pressure when you squeeze it gently end to end.

BANANAS: Use bananas to thicken drinks, and choose ripe or overripe bananas for maximum sweetness.

BASIL: Pair with peaches, strawberries, and other fruit for drinks and ices with an herbal twist.

BERRIES: For the best, fruit-forward flavor, use in-season or fresh frozen berries.

CARROTS: This veggie blends well with apples, oranges, tangerines, coconut, ginger, and peanuts. For the best flavor, choose young (not baby) carrots that are free of cracks and have fresh-looking greenery.

COCOA: There are two kinds of cocoa: Dutch-process cocoa has a mellow flavor, and natural cocoa is slightly bitter. Recipes in *Cooking Light Chill* were tested with natural cocoa.

CUCUMBERS: Seedless English cucumbers add a hint of refreshing herbal flavor to drinks and ices—and pairs well with fruit and herbs.

GINGER: Ginger complements both fruit and vegetables.

GRAPES: Frozen seedless grapes are an easy way to add sweetness to a drink or ice. Their flavor is mild enough to let other ingredients shine.

LEMONGRASS: Lemongrass adds a refreshing note to sweet treats. Use the white part of the stalk, but remove any pieces before serving—lemongrass is tough to chew.

MINT: Fresh mint goes well with many fruits and vegetables, as well as with chocolate. Steep the leaves to extract flavor, or add them to a drink or ice before processing.

PINEAPPLE: Use pineapple to add a tropical note to beverages. Core it and cut it into chunks. Follow the recipe for smooth results; pineapple's fibrous texture can make achieving the right texture tricky.

THYME: Try thyme with peaches, lemons, and oranges. Wrap fresh thyme in a paper towel and store it in a zip-top plastic bag in the refrigerator for up to a week.

TOMATOES: Tomatoes mix well with other fruits, including strawberries, watermelon, and peaches. Store tomatoes in a cool room—refrigeration will damage their flavor.

WATERMELON: Use cut, seedless watermelon in smoothies, juices, and ices. Most recipes call for it fresh, not frozen.

make treats naturally sweet

The key to sweetening a drink or ice naturally is to find ingredients that dissolve and freeze well. Some sweeteners boost flavor and texture.

CONCENTRATED JUICE: Frozen fruit juice concentrate allows you to add flavor, sweetness, and texture at one time.

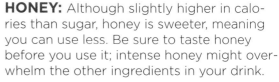

HONEY: Although slightly higher in calories than sugar, honey is sweeter, meaning you can use less. Be sure to taste honey before you use it; intense honey might overwhelm the other ingredients in your drink.

MAPLE SYRUP: Maple syrup is available in different grades—the lighter the color, the milder the flavor. Whichever you buy, be sure the label says "pure maple syrup"; syrups labeled "maple flavored" are usually a mix of corn syrup and artificial flavoring.

SIMPLE SYRUP: Simple syrup, made of equal parts of sugar and water, is the best way to use granulated sugar in a drink or ice: It's dissolved, so graininess won't be an issue.

SWEETENED CONDENSED MILK: The viscous consistency of sweetened condensed milk gives smoothies and ice creams a luxurious mouthfeel and prevents gritty crystallization from occurring.

add taste & texture
with nut & seed butters

There's a lot to love about these butters—they blend smoothly, and add nutty flavor to a drink. They also create creamy texture and a dose of healthy fats to a smoothie or shake.

ALMOND BUTTER: Mild and sweet, almond butter won't overwhelm other ingredients.

CASHEW BUTTER: Cashew butter has a luscious texture, with a buttery, sweet taste. It pairs nicely with coconut, ginger, and tropical fruits.

HAZELNUT BUTTER: This grainy, thick butter with brown specks is fruity and naturally sweet. Even though hazelnut butter has a distinct flavor, it pairs well with other ingredients, like apples, pears, and chocolate.

MACADAMIA BUTTER: Buttery-tasting and mild, this butter is fairly thin because of the high amount of healthy fats in the nuts. Chill it to keep it thick.

PEANUT BUTTER: Because of its assertive flavor, use peanut butter where it can be the star, or as part of a winning combo.

PECAN BUTTER: Pecan butter has a rich, hearty flavor. Pecan skins give the butter a slightly bitter aftertaste, so pair it with sweet ingredients.

SUNFLOWER SEED BUTTER: An alternative for people with peanut and tree-nut allergies, sunflower seed butter has a rich taste—use it when you want an assertive flavor.

TAHINI (SESAME SEED BUTTER): Made from ground sesame seeds, tahini is another option for people who have tree-nut allergies. Look for tahini made with toasted sesame seeds for stronger flavor.

go dairy-free

Can't do dairy? Don't let that limit you. Try these milks as an alternative to cow's milk in recipes.

1. ALMOND MILK: Nutty and toasty with slightly bitter undertones, this milk is made from ground almonds mixed with water. The mixture is filtered, then fortified with nutrients and thickened with agents like lecithin and carrageenan for body.

60 calories per cup; 0g sat fat, 1g protein

2. HEMP MILK: Made from seeds of the hemp plant, this milk is a bit chalky, with a strong, fermented, vitamin-like flavor. It is likely to be cloudy with particles, even when thickeners are added.

100 calories per cup; 0.5g sat fat, 3g protein

3. RICE MILK: Tastes just like sweet rice, and gets what little body it has from a small amount of safflower or canola oil.

120 calories per cup; 0g sat fat, 1g protein

4. SOY MILK: Most soy milks have added thickeners to get that rich, milk-like consistency—the benchmark for dairy substitutions. It is mildly nutty and creamy with a vegetal note.

80 calories per cup; 0g sat fat,
6g to 8g protein

5. COCONUT MILK: Similar to canned light coconut milk, but the smooth dairy-case kind has less sweet coconutty flavor and body.

80 calories per cup; 5g sat fat, 1g protein

STEP #3:
USE SMART TECHNIQUES

juice without a juicer

You don't need an expensive juicing machine to make your own juices— but you do need to know a few simple secrets. Fibrous ingredients like pineapple and mango can create juice with stringy textures; other fruits contribute pulp. Here's a simple way to get smooth results:

STEP 1: Place ingredients into blender according to recipe order.

STEP 2: Blend, scraping sides occasionally, until well blended.

STEP 3: Strain juice through a colander for a smooth texture.

STEP 4: Stir in water to achieve desired consistency.

blend a velvety drink

Making smooth smoothies and creamy shakes isn't as easy as it might seem: Some ingredients can leave behind chunks or get caught under the blades in your blender. Follow these fail-proof steps for luscious drinks:

STEP 1: Liquid ingredients should go into the blender first, closest to the blades. This allows the blending liquids to swirl and incorporate all of the other ingredients, preventing clumps.

STEP 2: Add the next softest ingredients. Blend 20 to 30 seconds before stopping to scrape down the sides of the blender to make sure everything is mixing evenly.

STEP 3: Add ice or other solid ingredients gradually as the blended mixture is flowing. Most blenders have a removable cap in the top lid that allows for easy access while blending.

TIP: If you want to make more servings, don't double the recipe—you may overfill the blender and have trouble getting smooth results. Instead, make another batch. Similarly, if you want less, don't try to downsize the recipe—you may not have enough ingredients for the blender to process properly. Follow the recipe and freeze the leftovers.

freeze your fruit for thicker drinks

Frozen fruit creates a thick texture and a cold drink. Freezing your own fruit gives you a chance to use great-tasting seasonal fruit in smoothies and drinks all year round. The best candidates are bananas, berries, and stone fruit such as cherries, peaches, and plums.

STEP 1: Wash the fruit and pat dry, then peel and remove pits if necessary. Cut large fruit into pieces.

STEP 2: Arrange the fruit on a baking sheet in a single layer, and freeze until the fruit is hard.

STEP 3: Transfer the fruit to a zip-top plastic bag. Store in small batches, and squeeze out as much air as you can as you seal the bag. You want the fruit to be tightly wrapped.

make frozen treats without an ice cream maker

Granitas are a low-tech way to create a frozen treat: You don't need an ice-cream freezer to make them. Follow these easy steps:

STEP 1: Follow recipe to make sweetened syrup. Pour syrup into an 11 x 7–inch glass or ceramic baking dish.

STEP 2: Cover and freeze on a level surface for about 45 minutes, or until the edges begin to ice.

STEP 3: Scrape with a small fork to start making small, jewel-like ice crystals.

STEP 4: Repeat process 3 more times, scraping every 45 minutes, or until completely frozen (about 3 hours). Remove from freezer; scrape until fluffy. Garnish, if desired.

smoothies

Fuel up: Tasty, low-cal smoothies are a busy person's go-to for a quick breakfast or a post-workout energy boost.

avocado smoothie

Avocado adds luscious creaminess and loads of nutrients to this cool, refreshing Vietnamese specialty. It's best served icy cold, straight from the blender.

1   ripe avocado

2   cups sweetened almond milk

1   cup crushed ice

¼   cup fat-free sweetened condensed milk

2   tablespoons fresh lime juice

1   tablespoon chopped slivered almonds, toasted

1. Cut avocado in half lengthwise; discard pit. Scoop pulp from avocado halves into blender. Add almond milk and next 3 ingredients (through lime juice); process until smooth. Top each serving with toasted almonds. Serve immediately. Serves 5 (serving size: about ¾ cup smoothie and about ½ teaspoon almonds)

CALORIES 142; FAT 7.6g (sat 0.9g, mono 4.4g, poly 0.9g); PROTEIN 2.7g; CARB 17g; FIBER 3.3g; CHOL 2mg; IRON 0.4mg; SODIUM 79mg; CALC 129mg

to your health

Avocados give you a dose of heart-healthy nutrients: Their monounsaturated fats and fiber help lower cholesterol.

banana cream pie smoothie

For fun, instead of sprinkling crumbs on top of the smoothie, create a graham cracker rim by dipping the glasses in water and then into the graham cracker crumbs. If you're serving a crowd, repeat the recipe—don't risk overfilling the blender by doubling the ingredients.

1   cup frozen sliced ripe banana (about 1 large)

1   cup vanilla low-fat yogurt

½   cup 1% low-fat milk

2   tablespoons whole-wheat graham cracker crumbs (about ½ cookie sheet)

1   tablespoon nonfat dry milk

½   teaspoon vanilla extract

3   ice cubes (about ¼ cup)

1   teaspoon graham cracker crumbs

1. Place frozen banana and next 6 ingredients (through ice cubes) in a blender; process until smooth. Pour evenly into 2 glasses, and sprinkle with graham cracker crumbs. Serve immediately. Serves 2 (serving size: about 1 cup)

CALORIES 216; FAT 2.8g (sat 1.5g, mono 0.8g, poly 0.3g); PROTEIN 9.8g; CARB 39.3g; FIBER 1.9g; CHOL 9mg; IRON 0.4mg; SODIUM 145mg; CALC 315mg

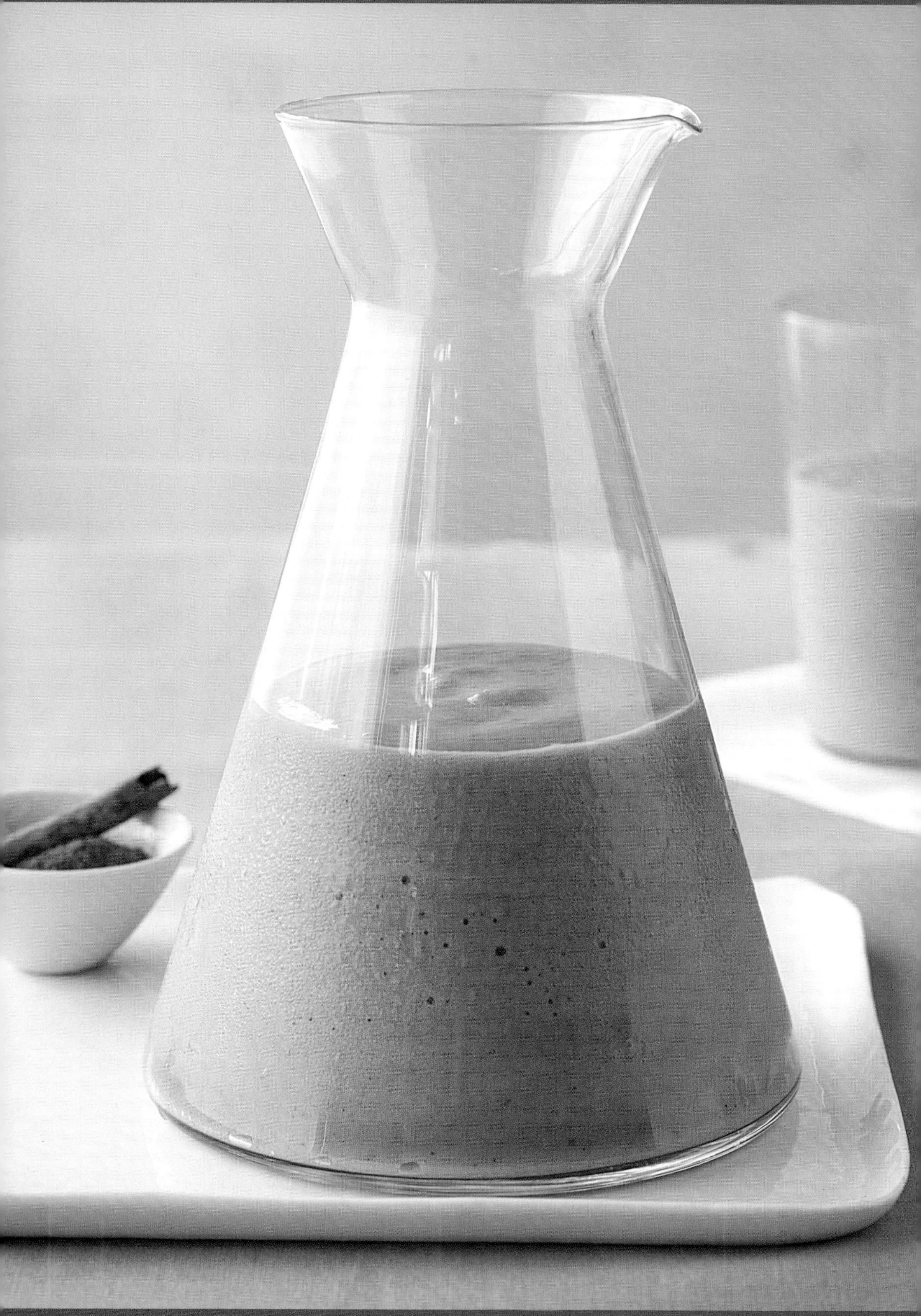

banana pumpkin smoothie

Frozen banana gives this pumpkin smoothie a thick texture; chilling the pumpkin ensures the smoothie stays cold when you blend it.

1   cup vanilla low-fat yogurt

¾   cup canned pumpkin, chilled

½   cup ice cubes

⅓   cup fresh orange juice (about 1 orange)

1   tablespoon brown sugar

½   teaspoon ground cinnamon

⅛   teaspoon ground nutmeg

Dash of ground cloves

1   frozen sliced ripe banana

Dash of ground cinnamon (optional)

1. Place yogurt and next 8 ingredients (through banana) in a blender; process until smooth. Garnish with dash of ground cinnamon, if desired. Serve immediately. Serves 2 (serving size: about 1 cup)

CALORIES 218; FAT 2.2g (sat 1.1g, mono 0.5g, poly 0.1g); PROTEIN 8.4g; CARB 44.5g; FIBER 5.5g; CHOL 6mg; IRON 1.2mg; SODIUM 87mg; CALC 243mg

berries and beets smoothie

Use either fresh or frozen raspberries; frozen fruit will help create a thicker texture. Look for cooked, peeled, ready-to-eat baby beets in the produce section.

1   **cup blueberries**

½   **cup fresh or frozen unsweetened raspberries**

⅓   **cup sliced, cooked beets**

¼   **cup plain fat-free Greek yogurt**

¼   **cup fresh orange juice**

1   **teaspoon honey**

1. Place all ingredients in a blender; process until smooth. Serves 1 (serving size: 1½ cups)

CALORIES 214; FAT 1g (sat 0g, mono 0.2g, poly 0.5g); PROTEIN 8g; CARB 47g; FIBER 8.9g; CHOL 0mg; IRON 1.3mg; SODIUM 59mg; CALC 76mg

berry and banana smoothie

If you like to tinker with smoothie recipes, this one is a great base to improvise from. Keep the banana and yogurt for texture.

- ½ **cup fresh orange juice (about 1 large orange)**
- 1¾ **cups plain fat-free Greek yogurt**
- 1 **tablespoon honey**
- 1 **frozen sliced banana**
- 1 **cup hulled strawberries**
- 1 **cup blackberries**

1. Place all ingredients in a blender; process until smooth. Serves 4 (serving size: about 1 cup)

CALORIES 138; FAT 0.4g (sat 0g, mono 0g, poly 0.2g); PROTEIN 9.8g; CARB 25.3g; FIBER 3.4g; CHOL 0mg; IRON 0.6mg; SODIUM 38mg; CALC 86mg

blackberry-mango breakfast smoothie

Sneak silken tofu into a sweet-tart breakfast smoothie. Combined with fiber-rich berries, this is a great way to get extra protein and fiber past pickier palates.

1½ cups frozen blackberries

1   cup refrigerated mango slices

1   cup (about 6½ ounces) low-fat silken tofu

1   cup orange juice

3   tablespoons honey

1. Place all ingredients in a blender; process until smooth. Serves 4 (serving size: 1 cup)

CALORIES 155; FAT 0.8g (sat 0.1g, mono 0.2g, poly 0.4g); PROTEIN 4g; CARB 35.9g; FIBER 3.7g; CHOL 0mg; IRON 1mg; SODIUM 39mg; CALC 44mg

to your health

Enjoy blackberries often to keep your brain healthy and your memory sharp. Blackberries are rich in polyphenols and flavonoids that accumulate and help boost your brain as you age.

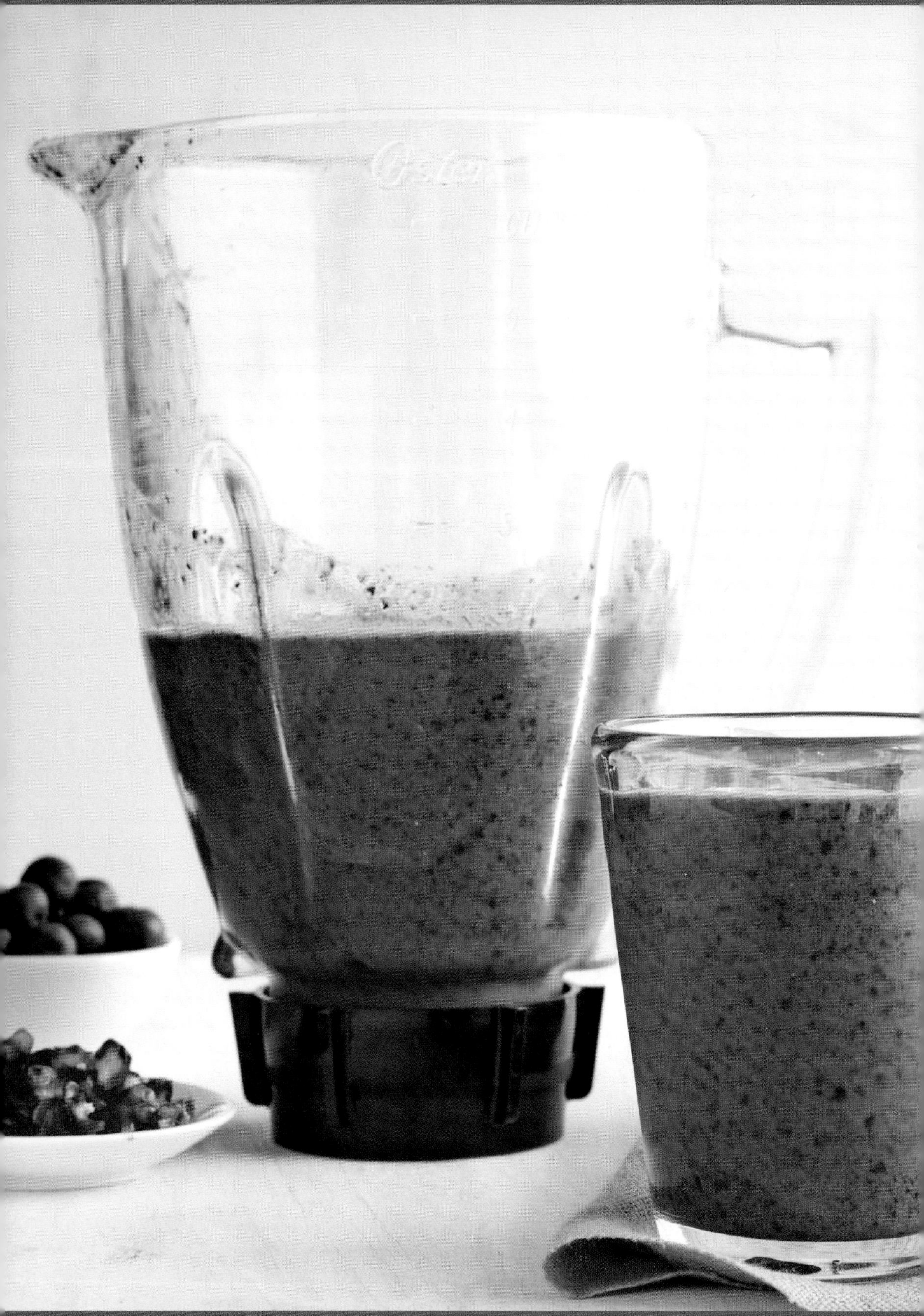
Oster

blueberry-pomegranate smoothie

Antioxidants found in both blueberries and pomegranates can help your body fight aging, cancer, and heart disease.

2   cups frozen blueberries

1   cup 100% pomegranate juice, chilled

1   tablespoon honey

1   (6-ounce) carton vanilla fat-free yogurt

1. Place all ingredients in a blender; process until smooth. Serves 4 (serving size: ⅔ cup)

CALORIES 116; FAT 0.5g (sat 0g, mono 0.1g, poly 0.2g); PROTEIN 2.3g; CARB 26.8g; FIBER 2.1g; CHOL 0mg; IRON 0.3mg; SODIUM 37mg; CALC 92mg

to your health

Smoothies like this, with protein and honey, make an ideal post-workout drink—the combo helps your muscles recover after exercise.

blueberry power smoothie

Choosing frozen blueberries over fresh will make a more vibrant-colored smoothie.

1   cup fresh or frozen blueberries

⅔   cup fat-free milk

½   cup reduced-fat firm silken tofu (about 4 ounces)

2   tablespoons raspberry spread

1   (6-ounce) carton raspberry low-fat yogurt

1. Place all ingredients in a blender; process until smooth. Serves 2 (serving size: 1¼ cups)

CALORIES 202; FAT 1.3g (sat 0.6g, mono 0.1g, poly 0.3g); PROTEIN 9.4g; CARB 38.2g; FIBER 2.3g; CHOL 6mg; IRON 1.6mg; SODIUM 134mg; CALC 231mg

check your chill IQ

Smoothie King's 20-ounce Blueberry Heaven has about the same amount of sodium as _____?

A. A 1.75-ounce bag of Planters Salted Peanuts (170 mg)
B. A 1.9-ounce bag of Lay's Sweet Southern Heat Barbecue Flavored Potato Chips (280 mg)
C. A 5-cup serving of Orville Redenbacher's Kettle Korn (130 mg)
D. 2 ounces of Baked! Cheetos (300 mg)

Answer: B. Smoothie King's 20-ounce Blueberry Heaven contains 259 mg sodium.

caramel espresso smoothie

For a thicker smoothie, make sure the tofu is cold.

¾ cup vanilla light soy milk

2 tablespoons fat-free caramel topping

6 ounces light silken tofu, drained and chilled

1 (.93-ounce) packet iced coffee–flavored instant coffee

1½ cups ice cubes

1. Place first 4 ingredients in a blender; process until smooth. Add ice cubes, a few at a time; process until thick. Serves 2 (serving size: 1½ cups)

CALORIES 156; FAT 1.5g (sat 0.3g, mono 0.3g, poly 0.8g); PROTEIN 8.4g; CARB 26g; FIBER 0.1g; CHOL 0mg; IRON 1.5mg; SODIUM 177mg; CALC 161mg

chocolate-almond banana smoothie

1 cup frozen sliced ripe banana (about 1 large)

½ cup chocolate almond milk

3 tablespoons almond butter

4 teaspoons chocolate-flavored malted milk powder

3 ice cubes

1. Place first 4 ingredients in a blender; process until smooth. Remove center cap from blender lid; secure lid on blender. With blender on, add ice cubes, 1 at a time, through center of blender lid, processing until smooth. Serves 2 (serving size: about ¾ cup)

CALORIES 276; FAT 12.9g (sat 1.2g, mono 7.9g, poly 3.4g); PROTEIN 7.2g; CARB 37g; FIBER 5.7g; CHOL 0mg; IRON 0.7mg; SODIUM 65mg; CALC 62mg

creamy cantaloupe smoothie

Choose a cantaloupe with a sweet fragrance for the best flavor.

- ½ **cup 1% low-fat milk**
- 2 **tablespoons honey**
- ½ **teaspoon grated lime rind**
- 1 **(5.3-ounce) carton vanilla fat-free Greek yogurt**
- 2½ **cups (1-inch) cubed peeled cantaloupe, frozen**

1. Place first 4 ingredients in a blender; process until smooth.

2. Remove center piece of blender lid; secure lid on blender. With blender on, drop cantaloupe cubes, 1 at a time, through center of blender lid; process until smooth. Serve immediately. Serves 2 (serving size: 1½ cups)

CALORIES 211; FAT 1g (sat 0.5g, mono 0.2g, poly 0.2g); PROTEIN 10.9g; CARB 42.4g; FIBER 1.7g; CHOL 3mg; IRON 0.5mg; SODIUM 93mg; CALC 92mg

creamy mango, avocado, and lime smoothie

¼ cup sliced avocado

1 cup sliced Champagne mango

1 tablespoon lime juice

1 tablespoon mint

1 teaspoon honey

2 cups crushed ice

Mint sprigs (optional)

1. Place ingredients in a blender; process until smooth. Garnish with mint sprig, if desired. Serves 1 (serving size: 1⅔ cups)

CALORIES 184; FAT 6g (sat 0.9g, mono 3.8g, poly 0.8g); PROTEIN 2.2g; CARB 35g; FIBER 5.2g; CHOL 0mg; IRON 0.6mg; SODIUM 5mg; CALC 29mg

dark cherry smoothie

For a dairy-free version, substitute vanilla-flavored cultured coconut-milk yogurt for the plain fat-free yogurt.

1½ **cups plain fat-free yogurt**

¼ **cup honey**

1 **(12-ounce) package frozen pitted dark sweet cherries**

1. Place yogurt in blender. Add honey and cherries; process until smooth. Serve immediately. Serves 4 (serving size: ¾ cup)

CALORIES 173; FAT 0g (sat 0g, mono 0g, poly 0g); PROTEIN 5g; CARB 43g; FIBER 0.6g; CHOL 1.9mg; IRON 0.3mg; SODIUM 51mg; CALC 126mg

fresh peach smoothie

When peach season is in full swing and the fruit is at its juicy-sweet best, get an extra basket or two to slice and freeze. You'll be ready to make this peaches-and-cream–like smoothie.

- ¾ cup peach nectar
- 1 tablespoon honey
- ⅛ teaspoon almond extract
- 2 (5.3-ounce) cartons vanilla fat-free Greek yogurt
- 3 cups sliced fresh peaches, frozen

Mint sprigs (optional)

1. Place first 4 ingredients in a blender; process until blended. Add peaches; process until smooth. Divide evenly among 4 glasses; garnish each serving with a mint sprig, if desired. Serve immediately. Serves 4 (serving size: 1 cup)

CALORIES 140; FAT 0.3g (sat 0g, mono 0.1g, poly 0.1g); PROTEIN 8.3g; CARB 27.6g; FIBER 2g; CHOL 0mg; IRON 0.4mg; SODIUM 37mg; CALC 10mg

ginger, berries, and oats smoothie

Ginger adds a touch of warmth to the fruit and honey in this smoothie. Store ginger tightly wrapped in the freezer; it will grate easily.

¼ cup prepared oatmeal

¼ cup 1% low-fat milk

½ teaspoon grated peeled fresh ginger

1 cup fresh blackberries

½ cup sliced strawberries

1 teaspoon honey

½ cup ice

1. Place ingredients in a blender; process until smooth. Serves 1 (serving size: 1¾ cups)

CALORIES 176; FAT 2.4g (sat 0.6g, mono 0.5g, poly 0.8g); PROTEIN 6g; CARB 36g; FIBER 9.9g; CHOL 3mg; IRON 4.8mg; SODIUM 58mg; CALC 179mg

go-getter green smoothie

Be sure to try this smoothie in the summer when honeydew melon is at its peak. Garnish glasses with wheels of additional peeled, sliced kiwifruit, if desired.

½   **cup vanilla light soy milk**

1   **(5.3-ounce) carton fat-free Greek yogurt with honey**

1   **cubed peeled kiwifruit**

1   **cup (½-inch) cubed honeydew melon**

1   **cup bagged baby spinach**

1   **cup sliced ripe banana, frozen (about 1 large)**

1. Place all ingredients in a blender; process until smooth. Serve immediately. Serves 2 (serving size: 1½ cups)

CALORIES 224; FAT 1.1g (sat 0.2g, mono 0.2g, poly 0.5g); PROTEIN 9.4g; CARB 47.9g; FIBER 4.3g; CHOL 0mg; IRON 1mg; SODIUM 91mg; CALC 180mg

grapefruit, fennel, and avocado smoothie

Avocado, grapefruit, and fennel are a popular salad trio; here's a drinkable version. Skewer extra apple and avocado slices for a pretty garnish, if desired.

2   cups fresh grapefruit juice (5 grapefruit)

1½ cups chopped fennel

1½ cups (½-inch) peeled Gala apple chunks

½   cup diced peeled avocado (1 small)

3   tablespoons honey

2   tablespoons chopped fennel fronds

1. Place all ingredients in a blender; process until smooth. Serve immediately. Serves 4 (serving size: 1 cup)

CALORIES 162; FAT 3.4g (sat 0.4g, mono 2.2g, poly 0.4g); PROTEIN 2.1g; CARB 33.9g; FIBER 3.9g; CHOL 0mg; IRON 1.2mg; SODIUM 22mg; CALC 67mg

green tea, kiwi, and mango smoothie

2½ cups frozen diced mango

¾ cup vanilla fat-free yogurt, divided

¼ cup honey, divided

2 tablespoons water

½ teaspoon grated lime rind

3 ripe kiwifruit, peeled and quartered

2 cups ice cubes

½ cup packed baby spinach

2 tablespoons bottled green tea

1. Place mango, ½ cup yogurt, 2 tablespoons honey, 2 tablespoons water, and lime rind in a blender; process until smooth, stirring occasionally. Divide half of mango mixture evenly among each of 4 glasses; place glasses in freezer. Set aside remaining mango mixture.

2. Rinse blender container. Place ¼ cup yogurt, 2 tablespoons honey, kiwifruit, and next 3 ingredients (through green tea) in blender; process until smooth, stirring occasionally. Gently spoon green tea–kiwi mixture over mango mixture in chilled glasses, working carefully around inside of each glass to create a clean horizontal line. Top green tea–kiwi mixture with remaining half of mango mixture. Stir to combine flavors, if desired. Serve immediately. Serves 4 (serving size: 1 cup)

CALORIES 234; FAT 0.4g (sat 0.1g, mono 0.1g, poly 0.2g); PROTEIN 3.2g; CARB 59.3g; FIBER 2.8g; CHOL 1mg; IRON 0.5mg; SODIUM 58mg; CALC 107mg

to your health

Spinach and other leafy greens like kale and Swiss chard are brimming with fiber, vitamins, minerals, and a variety of healthy plant-based nutrients that protect you from heart disease, diabetes, and cancer.

island sunrise smoothie

Play with your food: Have fun and serve smaller portions in hollowed-out limes.

- 2   cups chopped papaya
- ½   cup orange juice
- 1   tablespoon honey
- 2   teaspoons fresh lime juice

Pinch of salt

- 1   cup frozen (½-inch) cubed mango
- 1   cup frozen strawberries

1. Place first 5 ingredients in a blender; process until smooth. Add mango and strawberries; process until smooth. Serves 3 (serving size: 1 cup)

CALORIES 131; FAT 0.7g (sat 0.2g, mono 0.2g, poly 0.2g); PROTEIN 1.6g; CARB 32.7g; FIBER 3.6g; CHOL 0mg; IRON 0.6mg; SODIUM 59mg; CALC 39mg

to your health

Papayas are full of potassium—just what you need to avoid muscle cramps after a workout. Potassium helps keep your blood pressure on an even keel, too.

key lime-coconut smoothie

A cross between Key lime pie and a coconut mojito, this smoothie makes a great breakfast drink or sweet afternoon treat. Sprinkle some shredded coconut on top, if you like.

½   cup coconut milk

¼   teaspoon grated lime rind

1   tablespoon fresh lime juice

1   tablespoon honey

1   (6-ounce) carton Key lime fat-free yogurt, frozen

3   ice cubes

1. Place first 4 ingredients in a blender; process until smooth. Add yogurt; process until smooth. Remove center piece of blender lid; secure lid on blender. With blender on, drop ice cubes, 1 at a time, through center of blender lid; process until smooth. Serve immediately. Serves 2 (serving size: ¾ cup)

CALORIES 104; FAT 1.3g (sat 1.3g, mono 0g, poly 0g); PROTEIN 2.8g; CARB 20.4g; FIBER 0g; CHOL 1.5mg; IRON 0mg; SODIUM 51mg; CALC 102mg

mango lassi

Lassis are popular drinks in India, where they are made with yogurt or buttermilk. They should be light and frothy.

1   **cup chopped fresh mango**

1½   **tablespoons sugar**

1½   **cups plain fat-free Greek yogurt**

½   **cup 1% low-fat milk**

2   **teaspoons chopped pistachios**

Dash of ground cardamom (optional)

1. Place mango and sugar in a blender; process until pureed. Add yogurt and milk; process until smooth. Serve with pistachios; sprinkle with cardamom, if desired. Serves 3 (serving size: 1 cup lassi and about ½ teaspoon pistachios)

CALORIES 137; FAT 1.4g (sat 0.4g, mono 0.6g, poly 0.3g); PROTEIN 7g; CARB 27.5g; FIBER 1.2g; CHOL 4mg; IRON 0.2mg; SODIUM 89mg; CALC 207mg

mango-licious smoothie

With a one-two punch of mango, this is a perfect blend for fans of this tropical fruit.

2 cups frozen mango

½ cup mango nectar

2 tablespoons honey

1 (5.3-ounce) carton vanilla fat-free Greek yogurt

1. Place all ingredients in a blender; process until smooth. Serve immediately. Serves 2 (serving size: 1 cup)

CALORIES 233; FAT 0.6g (sat 0.2g, mono 0.2g, poly 0.1g); PROTEIN 7.9g; CARB 52.3g; FIBER 2.6g; CHOL 0mg; IRON 0.5mg; SODIUM 33mg; CALC 79mg

mexican cocoa smoothie

The secret to the rich chocolate flavor in this smoothie: a scoop of dark chocolate sorbet and cocoa powder. A pinch of cinnamon gives it a Mexican twist.

1   cup vanilla light soy milk

1   cup dark chocolate sorbet

½   cup light silken tofu

1   tablespoon unsweetened cocoa

2   teaspoons honey

⅛   teaspoon ground cinnamon

⅛   teaspoon vanilla extract

6   ice cubes

1. Place all ingredients in a blender; process until smooth. Serve immediately. Serves 2 (serving size: 1¼ cups)

CALORIES 167; FAT 1.6g (sat 0.5g, mono 0.4g, poly 0.6g); PROTEIN 5.5g; CARB 31.8g; FIBER 2.1g; CHOL 0mg; IRON 1mg; SODIUM 196mg; CALC 166mg

orange, banana, and pineapple frappé

A frappé is similar to a fruit juice or other liquid smoothie, but it's made with a larger proportion of fruit than dairy. Garnish with a twist of orange zest, if desired. To skip the dairy, substitute vanilla cultured coconut milk for the low-fat yogurt.

2⅓ cups frozen sliced banana (about 3 medium bananas)

¾ cup pineapple juice

½ cup orange sections (about 1 large orange)

½ cup plain low-fat yogurt

1 tablespoon flaked sweetened coconut

2 tablespoons thawed orange juice concentrate

1 (8-ounce) can pineapple chunks in juice, undrained

1. Place all ingredients in a blender; process until smooth. Serve immediately. Serves 4 (serving size: 1 cup)

CALORIES 194; FAT 1.3g (sat 0.8g, mono 0.2g, poly 0.1g); PROTEIN 3.5g; CARB 45.7g; FIBER 3.8g; CHOL 1.8mg; IRON 0.6mg; SODIUM 28mg; CALC 90mg

to your health

Drinking fruit-based beverages in the morning will help keep you hydrated throughout the day—most fruits and veggies consist mainly of water, giving your body extra H_2O.

peach-mango smoothie

Top this with diced fresh peaches, if desired.

⅔ **cup frozen sliced peaches**

⅔ **cup frozen mango pieces**

⅔ **cup peach nectar**

1 **tablespoon honey**

1 **(6-ounce) carton organic peach fat-free yogurt**

1. Place all ingredients in a blender; process until smooth. Serve immediately. Serves 2 (serving size: 1 cup)

CALORIES 184; FAT 0.3g (sat 0.1g, mono 0.1g, poly 0.1g); PROTEIN 4.1g; CARB 44g; FIBER 2.4g; CHOL 2mg; IRON 0.4mg; SODIUM 50mg; CALC 107mg

peanut butter, banana, and flax smoothie

The PB&B combo gives these smoothies kid-pleasing flavor. If the mixture seems too thick, add another tablespoon or two of milk.

½   cup 1% low-fat milk

½   cup vanilla fat-free yogurt

2   tablespoons ground golden flaxseed

1   tablespoon creamy peanut butter

1   teaspoon honey

¼   teaspoon vanilla extract

1   ripe banana, sliced

1. Place all ingredients in a blender; process until smooth. Serves 2 (serving size: about ¾ cup)

CALORIES 229; FAT 8.4g (sat 1.7g, mono 2.8g, poly 3.5g); PROTEIN 9.2g; CARB 32g; FIBER 4g; CHOL 3mg; IRON 0.8mg; SODIUM 113mg; CALC 211mg

peanut butter–berry smoothie

Inspired by a childhood favorite, this drink is reminiscent of a peanut butter and jelly sandwich. Serve garnished with more berries, if desired.

¼	**cup 1% low-fat milk**	1	**cup fresh or frozen raspberries**
½	**medium-sized ripe banana, sliced**	½	**cup crushed ice**
1	**tablespoon creamy peanut butter**		

1. Place all ingredients in a blender; process until smooth. Serves 1 (serving size: 1⅓ cups)

CALORIES 236; FAT 9.6g (sat 2.2g, mono 4.1g, poly 2.8g); PROTEIN 8g; CARB 34g; FIBER 10.5g; CHOL 3mg; IRON 1.3mg; SODIUM 102mg; CALC 117mg

pineapple-ginger smoothie

1   cup refrigerated pineapple-orange juice

2   cups (1-inch) pineapple chunks, frozen

1   teaspoon grated peeled fresh ginger

2   (5.3-ounce) cartons vanilla fat-free Greek yogurt

1. Place all ingredients in a blender; process until smooth. Serves 3 (serving size: about 1 cup)

CALORIES 166; FAT 0.1g (sat 0g, mono 0g, poly 0.1g); PROTEIN 10.7g; CARB 31.2g; FIBER 1.6g; CHOL 0mg; IRON 0.3mg; SODIUM 52mg; CALC 14mg

to your health

Sore and stiff? Researchers have found that fresh ginger may help soothe muscles after a workout.

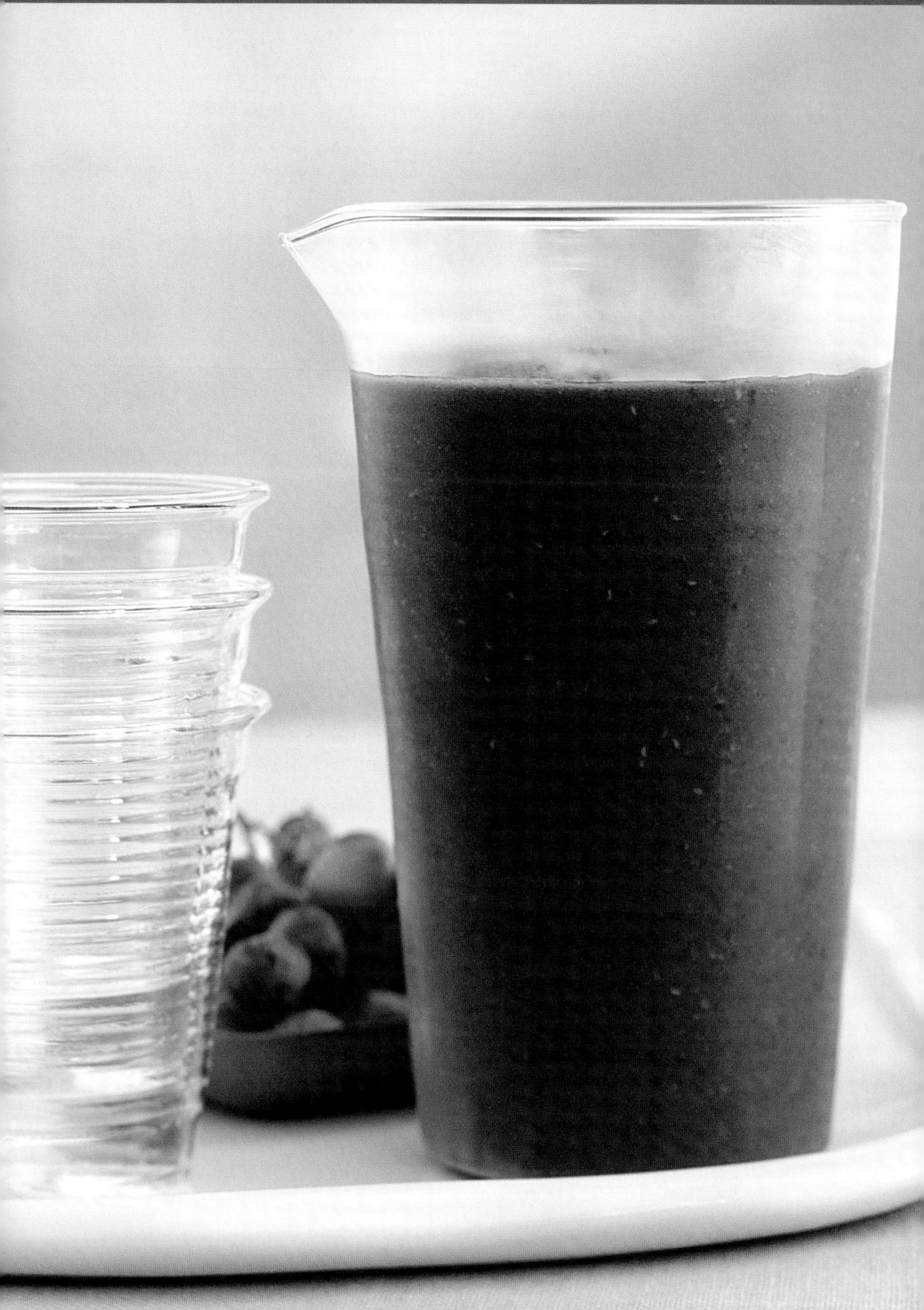

raspberry-grape smoothie

1   **cup frozen raspberries**

½   **cup refrigerated unsweetened 100% grape juice**

2   **tablespoons honey**

½   **teaspoon fresh lemon juice**

1   **(6-ounce) carton strawberry low-fat yogurt**

1. Place all ingredients in a blender; process until smooth. Serve immediately. Serves 2 (serving size: 1 cup)

CALORIES 208; FAT 0.8g (sat 0.5g, mono 0.2g, poly 0g); PROTEIN 3.2g; CARB 50.2g; FIBER 2.5g; CHOL 5mg; IRON 0.4mg; SODIUM 45mg; CALC 109mg

to your health

One cup of raspberries gives you half a day's dose of vitamin C and about a third of your daily fiber.

spiced chai frappé

This frappé is essentially the chilled version of a chai latte, perfect for an afternoon pick-me-up. Top each with a dollop of reduced-calorie whipped topping and a sprinkle of cinnamon, if desired.

½ **cup boiling water**

¼ **cup sugar**

4 **chai tea bags**

2 **cups ice**

½ **cup 1% reduced-fat milk**

1. Combine first 3 ingredients in a small bowl; cover and steep 5 minutes. Remove and discard tea bags. Refrigerate 30 minutes or until thoroughly chilled.

2. Place tea mixture, ice, and milk in a blender; process until smooth. Immediately pour frappé evenly into 2 glasses. Serves 2 (serving size: about 1 cup)

CALORIES 123; FAT 0.6g (sat 0.4g, mono 0.2g, poly 0g); PROTEIN 2.1g; CARB 30.2g; FIBER 0g; CHOL 3mg; IRON 0mg; SODIUM 27mg; CALC 73mg

spicy bloody mary smoothie

Enjoy the tangy, spicy flavor of a classic brunch drink without the alcohol.

1¾ cups low-sodium tomato juice, chilled

2 tablespoons fresh lemon juice

½ cup chopped English cucumber

2 teaspoons Worcestershire sauce

¾ teaspoon Sriracha (hot chile sauce)

5 ice cubes

3 (4-inch-long) English cucumber spears (optional)

1. Place all ingredients except cucumber spears in a blender; process until smooth. Pour into glasses. Garnish each serving with a cucumber spear, if desired. Serve immediately. Serves 3 (serving size: 1 cup)

CALORIES 37; FAT 0g (sat 0g, mono 0g, poly 0g); PROTEIN 1.3g; CARB 7.8g; FIBER 0.8g; CHOL 0mg; IRON 0.7mg; SODIUM 120mg; CALC 20mg

strawberry-guava smoothie

Look for guava nectar in the international section of your grocery store, or in specialty or Mexican markets.

1   cup quartered strawberries (about 5 ounces)

½   cup guava nectar

1   (6-ounce) carton organic strawberry fat-free yogurt

1   frozen sliced ripe banana

5   ice cubes (about 2 ounces)

1. Place all ingredients in a blender; process until smooth. Serve immediately. Serves 2 (serving size: 1 cup)

CALORIES 91; FAT 0.4g (sat 0.1g, mono 0g, poly 0.1g); PROTEIN 1g; CARB 21.6g; FIBER 1.4g; CHOL 0mg; IRON 2mg; SODIUM 16mg; CALC 41mg

strawberry-pineapple smoothie

Silken tofu and vanilla fro-yo make this smoothie creamy and add protein while keeping calories in check. Garnish the glass with a wedge of pineapple and a strawberry half, if desired.

⅔ cup silken tofu, drained (3 ounces)

1 cup cubed pineapple, frozen

1 cup sliced strawberries, frozen

½ cup vanilla low-fat frozen yogurt

⅓ cup orange juice

1 teaspoon sugar

1. Place all ingredients in a blender; process until smooth, scraping down sides. Serve immediately. Serves 4 (serving size: about 1 cup)

CALORIES 109; FAT 1.9g (sat 0.7g, mono 0.4g, poly 0.5g); PROTEIN 4g; CARB 20g; FIBER 1.5g; CHOL 16mg; IRON 0.5mg; SODIUM 16mg; CALC 83mg

skip the dairy

Substitute non-dairy vanilla frozen yogurt for the low-fat frozen yogurt.

triple melon smoothie

Melons are at their peak season June through September. Make this smoothie with ripe, in-season fruit for a great-tasting, refreshing drink when the weather's hot. Garnish with additional diced melon, if desired.

2½ cups chopped, seedless watermelon

½ cup orange juice

2 teaspoons honey

2½ cups (1-inch) cubed cantaloupe, frozen

1 cup (1-inch) cubed honeydew melon, frozen

1. Place first 3 ingredients in a blender; process until smooth.

2. Remove center piece of blender lid; secure blender lid on blender. With blender on, drop cantaloupe and honeydew through center of lid; process until smooth. Serves 4 (serving size: 1 cup)

CALORIES 102; FAT 0.5g (sat 0.1g, mono 0.1g, poly 0.2g); PROTEIN 1.9g; CARB 25.3g; FIBER 1.6g; CHOL 0mg; IRON 0.6mg; SODIUM 25mg; CALC 22mg

watermelon smoothie with a hint of mint

Use honey- or vanilla-flavored yogurt for a little extra sweetness. Garnish with a mint sprig, if desired.

2   **cups (1-inch) cubed seedless watermelon**

⅓   **cup plain 2% reduced-fat Greek yogurt**

2   **tablespoons chopped mint**

1. Place all ingredients in a blender; process until smooth. Serves 1 (serving size: about 1 cup)

CALORIES 143; FAT 2g (sat 1.1g, mono 0.5g, poly 0.2g); PROTEIN 8.3g; CARB 26.4g; FIBER 1.5g; CHOL 5mg; IRON 0.9mg; SODIUM 29mg; CALC 79mg

slushes & shakes

Try healthy versions of drive-thru favorites: slushes made with real fruit, and right-sized shakes for a creamy dessert.

almond, chocolate, and toasted coconut shake

This tasty dessert shake will remind you of a candy bar.

1¼ cups dark chocolate almond milk

2½ cups vanilla low-fat frozen yogurt

2 tablespoons maple syrup

2 tablespoons almond butter

⅛ teaspoon sea salt

2½ tablespoons flaked sweetened coconut, toasted

1. Place almond milk in a blender. Add frozen yogurt and next 3 ingredients (through sea salt); process until smooth. Pour into glasses; sprinkle with toasted coconut. Serves 5 (serving size: about ¾ cup)

CALORIES 302; FAT 9.5g (sat 3.5g, mono 3.7g, poly 1.2g); PROTEIN 11g; CARB 44g; FIBER 1.2g; CHOL 65mg; IRON 0.5mg; SODIUM 173mg; CALC 331mg

check your chill IQ

A medium Chocolate Hand Spun Shake from Burger King contains about the same amount of calories as _____?

A. 4 (1.25-oz.) packages cheese puffs (800 calories)
B. 1 large McDonald's French fries (500 calories)
C. 1 (3-oz.) package pork rinds (485 calories)
D. 2 slices pepperoni pizza (500 calories)

Answer: D. A Chocolate Hand Spun Shake contains 760 calories.

almond-tahini shake

This shake tastes like sesame candy because of the tahini—a thin, ground-up sesame seed paste that can be used in the same manner as peanut butter. Look for tahini made of hulled toasted sesame seeds for the best flavor.

½ cup vanilla almond milk

2 tablespoons tahini (roasted sesame seed paste)

2 whole pitted Medjool dates, chopped

Pinch of salt

1 cup vanilla almond milk dairy-free frozen dessert

Sesame candy (optional)

1. Place first 4 ingredients in a blender; process until smooth. Add frozen dessert; process until smooth. Garnish with a piece of sesame candy, if desired. Serves 2 (serving size: ¾ cup)

CALORIES 251; FAT 13.2g (sat 1.1g, mono 6.1g, poly 4.6g); PROTEIN 4g; CARB 35.5g; FIBER 6.5g; CHOL 0mg; IRON 0.8mg; SODIUM 199mg; CALC 75mg

apple cider slush

Honeycrisp apples, with their sweet-tart flavor, are the best choice for this slush. If you can't find them, look for Fuji apples as a stand-in.

4   cups ice cubes

2   cups 100% apple cider

1½ cups chopped peeled Honeycrisp apple (about 1 large)

2   tablespoons maple syrup

1   tablespoon lemon juice

1   teaspoon apple pie spice

6   thin Honeycrisp apple wedges

1. Place first 6 ingredients in a blender; process until slushy. Divide mixture among 6 glasses. Garnish each serving with 1 apple wedge. Serves 6 (serving size: 1 cup)

CALORIES 93; FAT 0.2g (sat 0.1g, mono 0g, poly 0g); PROTEIN 0.5g; CARB 23.6g; FIBER 0.9g; CHOL 0mg; IRON 0.1mg; SODIUM 1mg; CALC 10mg

black forest shake

This cake-inspired shake features grated chocolate—it's almost like eating a frozen chocolate-covered cherry.

3   cups chocolate light ice cream

½   cup 2% reduced-fat milk

¼   cup black cherry juice

½   ounce sweet baking chocolate, grated

10 frozen pitted dark sweet cherries

5   fresh dark sweet cherries (optional)

1. Place first 5 ingredients in a blender; process 1 minute or until smooth, scraping sides as necessary. Pour into 5 glasses. Garnish each serving with 1 fresh cherry, if desired. Serves 5 (serving size: about ¾ cup)

CALORIES 164; FAT 5.5g (sat 3.1g, mono 1.9g, poly 0.3g); PROTEIN 5g; CARB 26g; FIBER 0.5g; CHOL 20mg; IRON 1mg; SODIUM 12mg; CALC 103mg

skip the dairy

Omit the ice cream, milk, and sweet baking chocolate. Use equal amounts of chocolate almond milk ice cream and almond milk instead; replace the sweet baking chocolate with an equal amount of grated dairy-free chocolate.

blackberry shake

Rich in antioxidants, this brilliantly purple dairy-free shake makes for a healthful dessert. Oat milk is naturally sweet, but adding just a bit of honey really brings out the berries' flavor.

⅔   **cup blackberries**

½   **cup unsweetened oat milk**

½   **cup vanilla soy ice cream**

½   **teaspoon honey**

1. Place blackberries in a blender; process until pureed. Press puree through a sieve into a bowl to measure ¼ cup. Discard pulp and seeds.

2. Combine blackberry puree, oat milk, and remaining ingredients in a blender; process until smooth. Serve immediately. Serves 1 (serving size: 1¼ cups)

CALORIES 245; FAT 7.6g (sat 1.5g, mono 1.4g, poly 4.3g); PROTEIN 2.7g; CARB 43.1g; FIBER 5.1g; CHOL 0mg; IRON 1.1mg; SODIUM 145mg; CALC 52mg

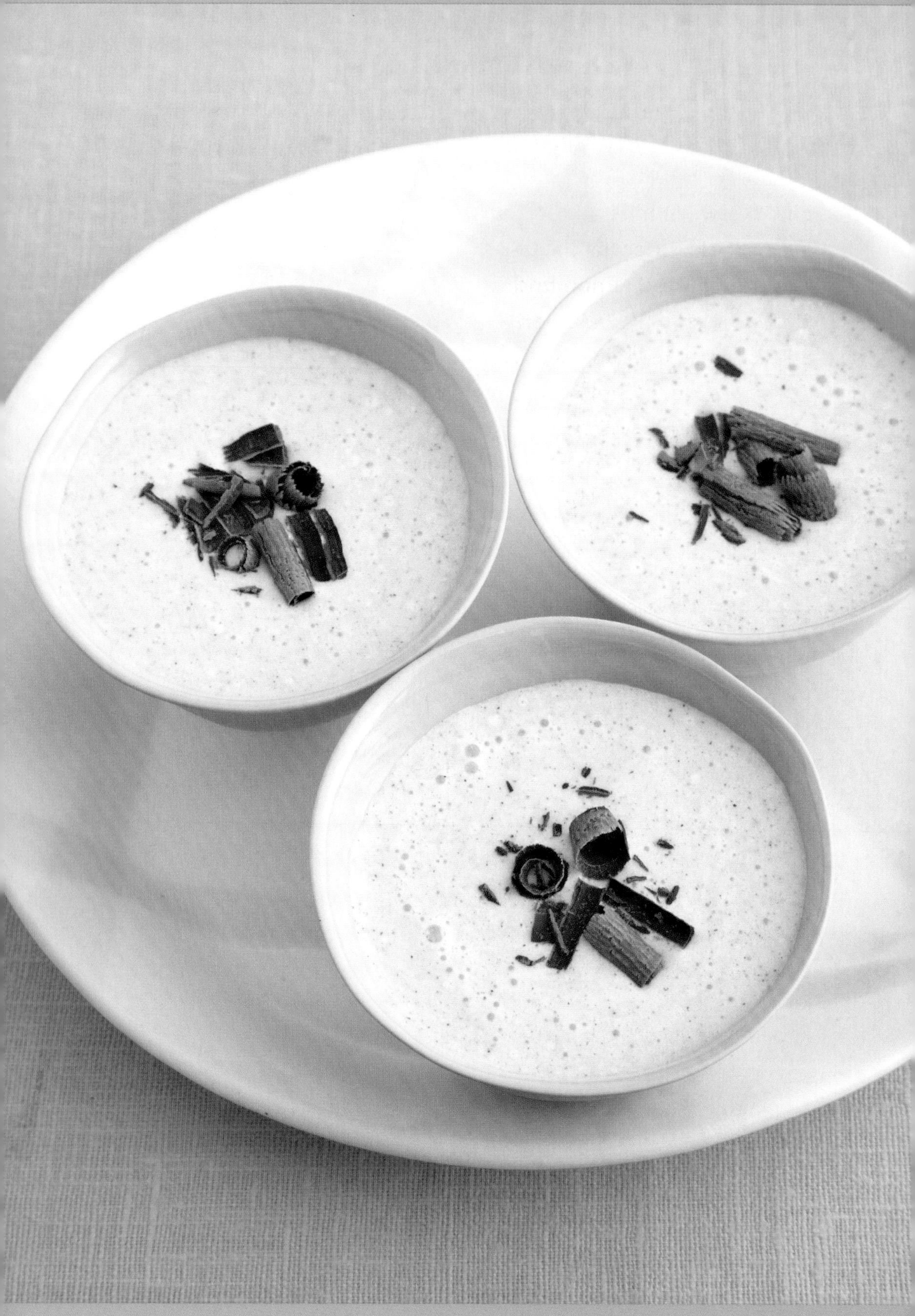

cannoli shake

The lovely flavors of sweet ricotta cheese, lemon, and cinnamon that we love in a cannoli are here in a luscious, calcium-rich shake. The dairy-free version tastes just as good.

¼   cup 1% low-fat milk

¼   cup part-skim ricotta cheese

½   teaspoon grated lemon rind

¼   teaspoon ground cinnamon

½   cup vanilla low-fat ice cream

½   teaspoon shaved bittersweet chocolate

1. Place first 5 ingredients in a blender in the order given; process until smooth. Pour into a glass, and sprinkle with shaved chocolate. Serve immediately. Serves 1 (serving size: 1 cup)

CALORIES 225; FAT 7.6g (sat 4.5g, mono 2.4g, poly 0.4g); PROTEIN 12.2g; CARB 26.1g; FIBER 1.5g; CHOL 27mg; IRON 0.4mg; SODIUM 149mg; CALC 353mg

skip the dairy

Substitute equal amounts of non-dairy tofu ricotta, unsweetened almond milk, and non-dairy tofu ice cream for the part-skim ricotta, low-fat milk, and low-fat ice cream.

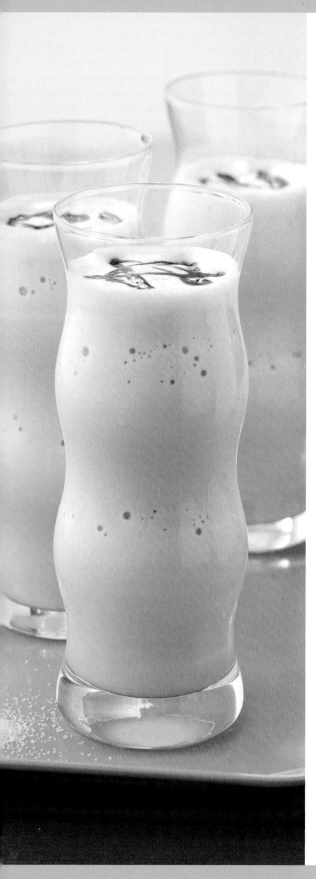

caramel–sea salt milk shake

Watch the sugar carefully: The darker it gets, the more flavor it develops, but it will burn quickly.

½   **cup sugar**

¼   **cup fat-free milk**

1½   **tablespoons butter**

1   **teaspoon sea salt**

3   **cups vanilla light ice cream**

1. Place sugar in a 2-quart heavy saucepan. Cook over medium heat 3 to 4 minutes or until a deep amber color. Remove pan from heat; add milk, butter, and salt (mixture will bubble vigorously). Return pan to heat. Cook, stirring constantly, until blended and smooth. Remove from heat; cool 3 minutes (do not allow caramel to harden). Reserve 2 tablespoons caramel sauce.

2. Place ice cream in a blender. Remove center piece of blender lid; secure blender lid on blender. With blender on, slowly pour caramel sauce into ice cream; process until smooth.

3. Pour ice cream mixture into 6 tall glasses. Drizzle reserved caramel sauce over milk shakes. Serves 6 (serving size: ⅔ cup milk shake and 1 teaspoon caramel sauce)

CALORIES 231; FAT 6.5g (sat 4g, mono 1.7g, poly 0.3g); PROTEIN 4g; CARB 40g; FIBER 0g; CHOL 28mg; IRON 0mg; SODIUM 473mg; CALC 136mg

cherry limeade slush

Here's a soda-shop favorite in a homemade icy slush.

2 cups lime-flavored sparkling water, chilled and divided

½ cup frozen limeade concentrate

1 (12-ounce) package frozen pitted dark sweet cherries

Lime slices (optional)

1. Place 1 cup sparkling water, limeade concentrate, and cherries in a blender; process until smooth. Pour cherry mixture into a pitcher. Gently stir in 1 cup sparkling water. Divide mixture among 4 glasses; garnish with lime slices, if desired. Serves 4 (serving size: 1 cup)

CALORIES 163; FAT 0g (sat 0g, mono 0g, poly 0g); PROTEIN 1.2g; CARB 41.5g; FIBER 0.6g; CHOL 0mg; IRON 0.2mg; SODIUM 23mg; CALC 12mg

frozen chocolate-banana shake

Love chocolate-dipped frozen bananas at the amusement park? Enjoy the same flavors in a glass. Tofu adds creaminess to this dessert shake.

1	cup chocolate-flavored dairy-free frozen dessert	½	cup silken tofu
1	cup chocolate light soy milk	1½	cups frozen sliced ripe banana (about 2 bananas)

1. Place all ingredients in a blender; process until smooth. Serves 3 (serving size: about 1 cup)

CALORIES 200; FAT 6g (sat 0.8g, mono 2.8g, poly 2.2g); PROTEIN 5g; CARB 39g; FIBER 9.4g; CHOL 0mg; IRON 1.4mg; SODIUM 73mg; CALC 244mg

chocolate-hazelnut milk shake

The combo of chocolate and hazelnut is mainstream in America, thanks to creamy spreads. Use a bit to flavor this dessert shake.

- **3 cups vanilla bean light ice cream**
- **½ cup 1% low-fat milk**
- **1½ tablespoons chocolate-hazelnut spread**
- **1 ounce semisweet chocolate baking bar, grated**
- **15 hazelnuts, toasted**

1. Place first 4 ingredients in a blender; process until smooth. Pour into 5 glasses. Garnish each serving with 3 hazelnuts. Serves 5 (serving size: ½ cup)

CALORIES 259; FAT 10.5g (sat 5.6g, mono 3.6g, poly 0.6g); PROTEIN 6.5g; CARB 36g; FIBER 1.3g; CHOL 26mg; IRON 0.6mg; SODIUM 81mg; CALC 188mg

date milk shake

Date milk shakes are a popular cool treat in sunny Southern California, where extremely large Medjool dates grow abundantly. Sprinkle each dessert shake with additional cinnamon, if desired.

- ½ **cup fat-free milk**
- 3 **pitted Medjool dates**
- 2 **cups vanilla fat-free ice cream**
- 1 **tablespoon flaxseed meal**
- ⅛ **teaspoon ground cinnamon**

1. Combine milk and dates in a blender; process until smooth. Add ice cream, meal, and cinnamon; process until blended. Serve immediately. Serves 3 (serving size: about ⅔ cup)

CALORIES 221; FAT 1g (sat 0g, mono 0.2g, poly 0.8g); PROTEIN 6g; CARB 50g; FIBER 2g; CHOL 1mg; IRON 0mg; SODIUM 77mg; CALC 171mg

skip the dairy

Substitute equal amounts of vanilla almond milk and vanilla almond milk dairy-free frozen dessert for the milk and ice cream.

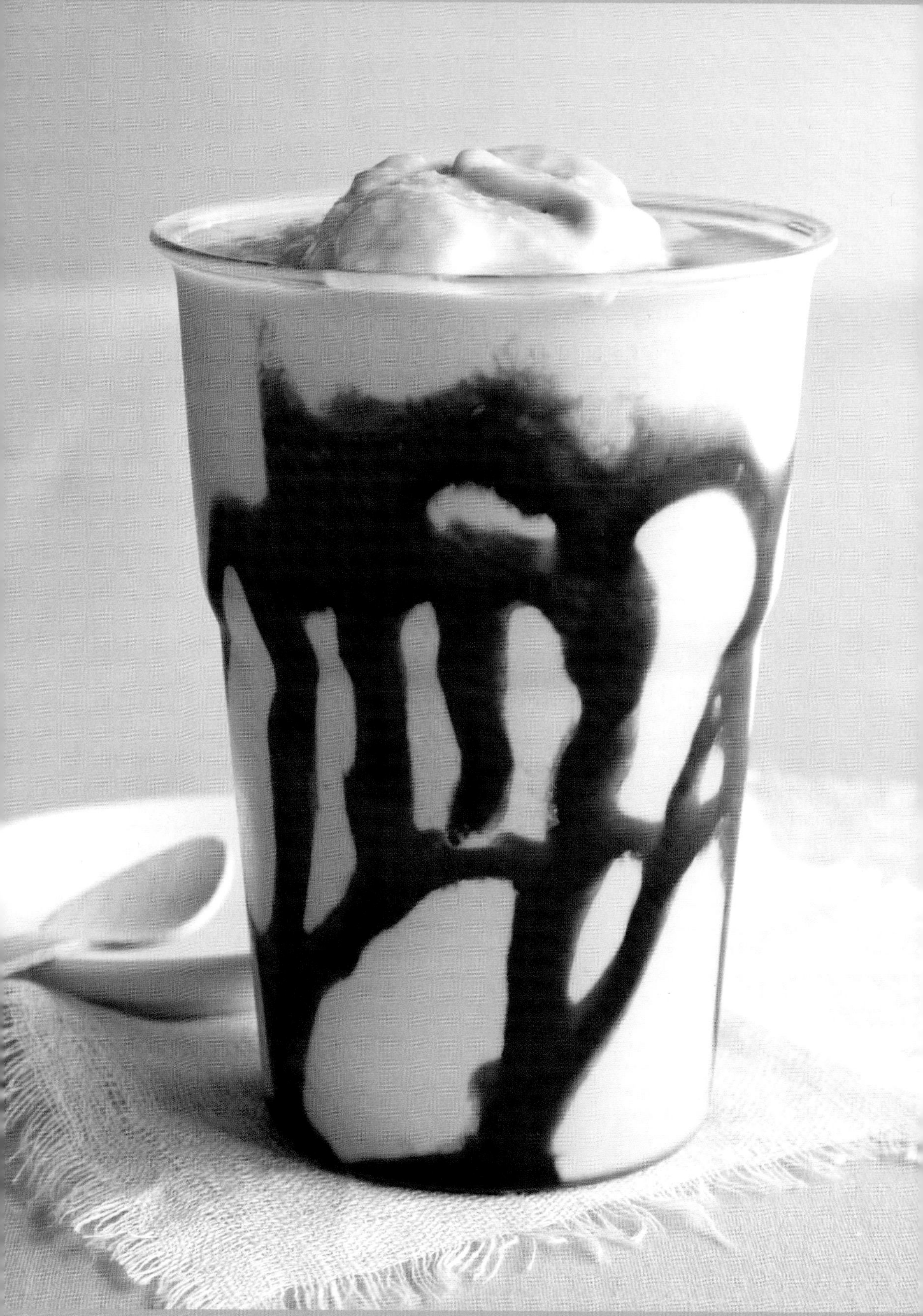

espresso–soy milk shake

This flavorful shake is a speedy dessert. It's also a sweet way to enjoy the health benefits of caffeine, which can boost your endurance in aerobic activities.

2 tablespoons fat-free chocolate syrup

2⅛ teaspoons instant espresso granules or instant coffee granules, divided

1½ cups vanilla soy ice cream

½ cup plain low-fat soy milk

1. Combine syrup and ⅛ teaspoon espresso granules in a small bowl, stirring well. Using a spoon, drizzle half of syrup mixture around the inside rim of 2 small narrow glasses. Combine 2 teaspoons espresso granules, ice cream, and milk in a blender; process until smooth. Pour 1 cup ice cream mixture into each of 2 glasses. Serve immediately. Serves 2 (serving size: 1 cup)

CALORIES 290; FAT 10.9g (sat 2.3g, mono 2.1g, poly 5.5g); PROTEIN 3.1g; CARB 43.9g; FIBER 1g; CHOL 0mg; IRON 0.9mg; SODIUM 243mg; CALC 81mg

skip the dairy

Use an equal amount of dairy-free chocolate syrup in place of the chocolate syrup.

frozen honeydew-limeade slush

4   cups (1-inch) cubed honeydew melon (about ½ melon)

2   cups fresh lime juice (about 12 limes)

2   cups lime sparkling water, chilled

1   cup sugar

½   cup mint leaves

4   cups sugar-free ginger ale, chilled

Lime slices (optional)

1. Freeze cubed honeydew at least 3 hours.

2. Place 2 cups frozen honeydew, 1 cup lime juice, 1 cup sparkling water, ½ cup sugar, and ¼ cup mint in a blender; process until smooth. Repeat procedure with remaining honeydew, lime juice, sparkling water, sugar, and mint.

3. Pour ½ cup ginger ale in bottom of each of 8 chilled glasses. Pour 1 cup honeydew mixture in each glass; stir gently. Garnish with lime slices, if desired. Serves 8 (serving size: 1½ cups)

CALORIES 146; FAT 0.2g (sat 0.1g, mono 0g, poly 0.1g); PROTEIN 0.9g; CARB 38.5g; FIBER 1.3g; CHOL 0mg; IRON 0.9mg; SODIUM 60mg; CALC 25mg

grasshopper mocha shake

Fresh mint, chocolate sorbet, and chocolate wafer cookies make this an intensely enjoyable mint-chocolate dessert.

¾ cup 2% reduced-fat milk

¼ cup half-and-half

1 (1-ounce) package mint

1 cup ice cubes

½ cup mocha–flavored hot cocoa powder

4 chocolate wafer cookies, broken

1 (14-ounce) container chocolate sorbet

1. Combine milk and half-and-half in a small saucepan. Bring to a simmer. Remove from heat; stir in mint. Place pan in a large ice-filled bowl; cool completely (about 10 minutes), stirring occasionally. Discard mint.

2. Place milk mixture, ice, and next 3 ingredients (through cookies) in a blender; process until smooth. Serves 4 (serving size: about ¾ cup)

CALORIES 259; FAT 4.5g (sat 2.7g, mono 1.1g, poly 0.2g); PROTEIN 5g; CARB 47g; FIBER 3g; CHOL 10mg; IRON 1mg; SODIUM 308mg; CALC 240mg

honey-peanut butter shake

Peanut butter, soy milk, honey, and frozen tofu yogurt blend into a thick, dairy-free treat. Swirl a small amount of extra honey on top, if desired.

1   cup light vanilla soy milk

⅓   cup cubed soft silken tofu

1   tablespoon creamy peanut butter

1   tablespoon honey

2   cups vanilla frozen tofu yogurt

1. Place first 4 ingredients in a blender; process until smooth. Add frozen tofu yogurt, and process until smooth. Serves 4 (serving size: ¾ cup)

CALORIES 276; FAT 16g (sat 2.5g, mono 4g, poly 8.4g); PROTEIN 4.7g; CARB 29.1g; FIBER 0.3g; CHOL 0mg; IRON 0.4mg; SODIUM 179mg; CALC 80mg

tasty twist

Use this recipe as a base shake that can work with other nut butters you have in your pantry—the other ingredients will complement any variety. Natural nut butters will produce a shake with a slightly different texture.

horchata shake

Horchata is a cinnamon-laced drink based on traditional agua frescas of Mexico and Guatemala. A frozen banana whirred up with the vanilla-flavored milk base creates a delicious shake.

1½ **cups unsweetened vanilla almond milk**

1½ **cups original rice milk**

1 **cup frozen sliced ripe banana (about 1 large banana)**

¼ **cup sugar**

½ **teaspoon ground cinnamon**

Ice cubes

1. Place first 5 ingredients in a blender; fill remainder of blender container with ice. Process until smooth. Serves 5 (serving size: 1 cup)

CALORIES 112; FAT 1.5g (sat 0g, mono 1g, poly 0.5g); PROTEIN 1g; CARB 25g; FIBER 1g; CHOL 0mg; IRON 0mg; SODIUM 81mg; CALC 71mg

lemongrass slush

Using lemongrass paste instead of lemongrass saves you time and delivers plenty of flavor. Combined with cucumber and honeydew, it makes a refreshing slush.

1 cup light coconut milk

1½ teaspoons grated lemon rind

¼ cup fresh lemon juice (about 2 lemons)

¼ cup honey

2 tablespoons refrigerated lemongrass paste

Dash of salt

3½ cups (1½-inch) cubed honeydew melon, frozen (about ½ melon)

1 cup coarsely chopped seeded peeled cucumber, frozen

1 cup ice cubes

½ cup ginger ale

1. Place first 8 ingredients (through cucumber) in a blender; process until smooth. Add ice, and process just until blended.

2. Divide mixture among 4 glasses. Top each serving with 2 table-spoons ginger ale. Serves 4 (serving size: 1 cup)

CALORIES 163; FAT 1.9g (sat 0.7g, mono 0g, poly 0.1g); PROTEIN 1.3g; CARB 38g; FIBER 1.6g; CHOL 0mg; IRON 0.4mg; SODIUM 270mg; CALC 17mg

maple-hazelnut shake

Make your own roasted hazelnut butter or use a store-bought version. For a dairy-free shake, use an equal amount of vanilla almond milk dairy-free frozen dessert instead of the ice cream.

1   **cup vanilla low-fat ice cream**

½   **cup unsweetened hazelnut milk, chilled**

1   **tablespoon maple syrup**

1   **tablespoon Hazelnut Butter (below)**

1. Place all ingredients in a blender; process until smooth. Serve immediately. Serves 2 (serving size: ⅔ cup)

CALORIES 196; FAT 7.5g (sat 1.4g, mono 4.9g, poly 0.8g); PROTEIN 5g; CARB 32g; FIBER 4g; CHOL 5mg; IRON 0.5mg; SODIUM 86mg; CALC 195mg

hazelnut butter

Save the remaining hazelnut butter to use as a sandwich or toast spread, or to enjoy with apple and pear wedges.

2   **cups hazelnuts**

1. Preheat oven to 275°.

2. Place hazelnuts on a jelly-roll pan. Bake at 275° for 20 minutes, stirring once. Turn nuts out onto a towel. Roll up towel; rub off skins. Let cool completely.

3. Place hazelnuts in a food processor; process 2 minutes or until a paste forms. Scrape mixture into a clean container with a rubber spatula; cover with lid and store in an airtight container in the refrigerator for up to 2 months. Serves 16 (serving size: 1 tablespoon)

CALORIES 106; FAT 10.3g (sat 0.8g, mono 7.7g, poly 1.3g); PROTEIN 2.5g; CARB 2.8g; FIBER 1.6g; CHOL 0mg; IRON 0.8mg; SODIUM 0mg; CALC 19mg

milk chocolate almond shake

⅓ cup unsweetened almond milk, chilled

½ cup vanilla almond milk ice cream

2 teaspoons unsweetened cocoa

⅛ teaspoon almond extract

1. Place all ingredients in a blender; process until smooth. Pour into a glass and serve immediately. Serves 1 (serving size: ¾ cup)

CALORIES 153; FAT 6g (sat 0.3g, mono 3.7g, poly 1.5g); PROTEIN 2g; CARB 28.7g; FIBER 6.5g; CHOL 0mg; IRON 0.6mg; SODIUM 136mg; CALC 71mg

mocha slush

The secret to the flavor of this slush: espresso ice cubes. You'll have extra, so keep the ice cubes in a zip-top freezer bag for a quick frozen coffee treat that's much healthier than a trip through the drive-thru. (Got leftover coffee? Freeze it into ice cubes to use in place of the espresso cubes.)

3   cups water

5   teaspoons instant espresso powder

¼   cup 1% low-fat chocolate milk

1   tablespoon chocolate syrup, divided

1. Combine 3 cups water and espresso powder. Pour espresso into 2 ice cube trays; freeze 4 hours or until firm.

2. Place 4 frozen coffee cubes, chocolate milk, and 1½ teaspoons chocolate syrup in a blender; process until slushy. Pour slush into a glass; swirl 1½ teaspoons chocolate syrup into the slush. Serve immediately. Serves 1 (serving size: 1¼ cups)

CALORIES 102; FAT 0.6g (sat 0.4g, mono 0.2g, poly 0g); PROTEIN 3.1g; CARB 20.1g; FIBER 0.5g; CHOL 2mg; IRON 0.2mg; SODIUM 64mg; CALC 81mg

orange cream shake

This will bring back memories of a familiar childhood ice cream treat on a stick! For an extra-special presentation, serve this shake in a hollowed orange.

1   cup vanilla light ice cream
½   cup orange sherbet
½   teaspoon grated orange rind
6   tablespoons fresh orange juice (about 1 orange)
¼   teaspoon vanilla extract

1. Place all ingredients in a blender; process until smooth. Serves 2 (serving size: ⅔ cup)

CALORIES 220; FAT 4.3g (sat 2.5g, mono 1.2g, poly 0.2g); PROTEIN 4.5g; CARB 40.4g; FIBER 0.4g; CHOL 23mg; IRON 0.2mg; SODIUM 74mg; CALC 148mg

papaya shake

When choosing papaya, look for fruit that gives slightly to pressure. If it isn't yet ripe, keep it in a sealed brown paper bag for a few days.

2   cups chopped papaya (about 1 papaya), frozen

1   cup chopped fresh pineapple, frozen

1   cup chopped peeled ripe peaches, frozen (1 large)

¾   cup peach nectar

¾   cup rice milk

2   tablespoons fresh lime juice

2   tablespoons maple syrup

Dash of sea salt

1. Place all ingredients in a blender; process until smooth. Serve immediately. Serves 4 (serving size: 1 cup)

CALORIES 146; FAT 0.5g (sat 0g, mono 0.3g, poly 0.1g); PROTEIN 0.9g; CARB 37.1g; FIBER 2.4g; CHOL 0mg; IRON 0.5mg; SODIUM 63mg; CALC 45mg

passion fruit-tea slush

Passion fruit juice can be found in many Latin American supermarkets.

1   **cup bottled unsweetened iced tea**

1   **cup passion fruit juice**

2   **cups ice cubes**

2   **tablespoons superfine sugar**

2   **large carambolas (star fruits), sliced**

1. Combine tea and juice in an 8-inch square glass or ceramic baking dish. Cover and freeze 1 hour or until slushy. Remove from freezer; combine tea mixture, ice, and sugar in a blender. Process until smooth. Garnish with a star fruit slice. Serves 6 (serving size: ⅔ cup)

CALORIES 53; FAT 0.2g (sat 0g, mono 0g, poly 0.1g); PROTEIN 0.7g; CARB 12.7g; FIBER 1.1g; CHOL 0mg; IRON 0.2mg; SODIUM 4mg; CALC 3mg

piña colada shake

Take a sip, close your eyes...and you're on a tropical island. Serve with pineapple wedges, if desired.

- 1½ **cups fresh pineapple cubes, frozen**
- 1½ **cups vanilla dairy-free frozen dessert**
- ½ **cup light coconut milk**
- ⅛ **teaspoon coconut extract**
- ¾ **cup frozen sliced banana (about 1 small banana)**

1. Place all ingredients in a blender; process until smooth. Serve immediately. Serves 4 (serving size: 1 cup)

CALORIES 155; FAT 2.7g (sat 0.3g, mono 0.7g, poly 1.5g); PROTEIN 1g; CARB 32g; FIBER 4g; CHOL 0mg; IRON 0.5mg; SODIUM 43mg; CALC 9mg

spicy pineapple slush

Use a glass baking dish to freeze the mixture; a metal pan can give the slush an off flavor. If you'd like a spicier slush, leave the seeds in the jalapeño and dip the rims of the glasses in water, then in ancho chile powder.

1¼ cups pineapple juice

1 teaspoon chopped seeded jalapeño pepper

2¼ cups fresh pineapple chunks

2 tablespoons fresh lime juice

2 tablespoons honey

1 tablespoon fat-free sweetened condensed milk

⅛ teaspoon salt

⅛ teaspoon ancho chile powder

1. Bring pineapple juice to a boil. Add jalapeño pepper; cover, reduce heat, and simmer 5 minutes. Strain pineapple mixture through a sieve into a bowl; discard solids. Let cool 25 minutes.

2. Place strained pineapple juice, pineapple chunks, and next 5 ingredients (through milk) in a blender; process until smooth.

3. Pour mixture into an 8-inch square glass or ceramic baking dish. Cover and freeze 3 hours or until mixture is slushy, removing from freezer and scraping entire mixture with a fork every 30 minutes.

4. Spoon pineapple mixture into 4 glasses. Serve immediately. Serves 4 (serving size: ⅔ cup)

CALORIES 136; FAT 0.2g (sat 0g, mono 0g, poly 0.1g); PROTEIN 1.3g; CARB 34.4g; FIBER 1.5g; CHOL 1mg; IRON 1mg; SODIUM 84mg; CALC 36mg

pumpkin pie shake

Canned pumpkin has more bio-available beta-carotene than fresh because of the heat used during canning. Dress up this shake with a rim of graham cracker crumbs on each glass instead of sprinkling the crumbs on the shake.

3   **cups vanilla reduced-fat ice cream, softened**

⅔   **cup canned pumpkin**

⅓   **cup fat-free milk**

¼   **cup packed brown sugar**

¾   **teaspoon pumpkin pie spice**

4   **teaspoons graham cracker crumbs (optional)**

3   **tablespoons frozen reduced-calorie whipped topping, thawed**

Pumpkin pie spice (optional)

1. Place first 5 ingredients in a blender; process until smooth. Pour ¾ cup ice cream mixture into each of 4 glasses. Top each with 1 teaspoon graham cracker crumbs, if desired, and about 2 teaspoons whipped topping. Sprinkle with additional pumpkin pie spice, if desired. Serves 4 (serving size: ¾ cup)

CALORIES 247; FAT 3.5g (sat 2g, mono 1g, poly 0.2g); PROTEIN 5.7g; CARB 47.7g; FIBER 2.7g; CHOL 8mg; IRON 1mg; SODIUM 82mg; CALC 200mg

rich pistachio shake

Satisfy your salty-sweet craving: Maple syrup and sea salt give this nutty dessert shake nuanced flavor. Garnish with additional chopped pistachios, if desired.

¾ **cup unsweetened almond milk**

⅓ **cup pistachios**

2 **tablespoons maple syrup**

⅛ **teaspoon vanilla extract**

Dash of coarse sea salt

2 **cups vanilla low-fat frozen yogurt**

1. Place first 5 ingredients in a blender; process until smooth.

2. Add frozen yogurt; process until smooth. Divide among 4 glasses. Serve immediately. Serves 4 (serving size: about ⅔ cup)

CALORIES 292; FAT 9.7g (sat 3.1g, mono 2.8g, poly 1.5g); PROTEIN 11.3g; CARB 41g; FIBER 1.2g; CHOL 65mg; IRON 0.5mg; SODIUM 169mg; CALC 309mg

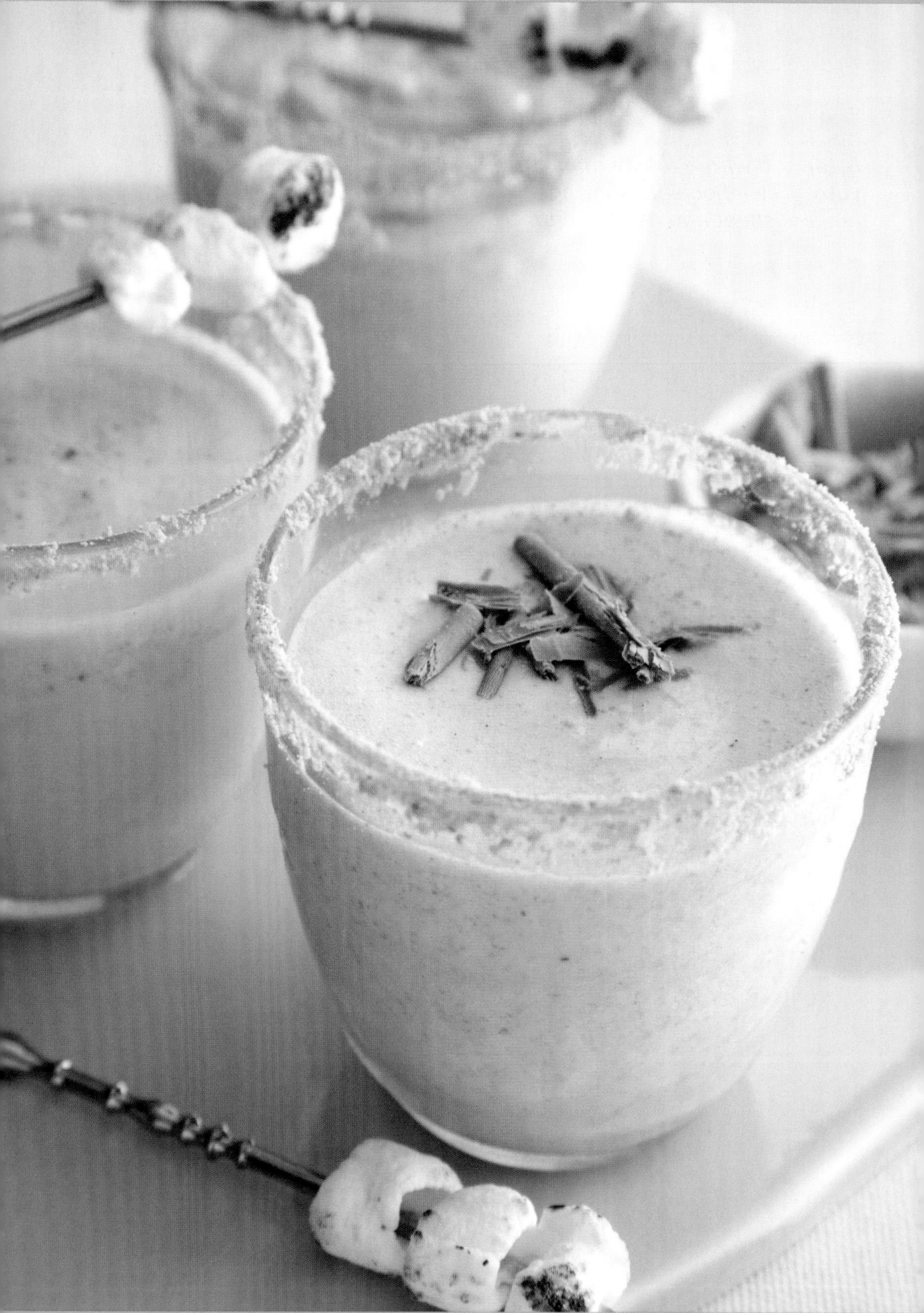

s'mores shake

A campfire dessert in a glass: Broiling marshmallows in the oven is a quick way to get the fire-toasted flavor you grew up with. Each shake is topped with a toasty marshmallow; if you like, sprinkle each shake with a few chocolate shavings. You can also crush another graham cracker sheet and use the crumbs to rim the glasses.

8   stackable marshmallows

4   graham cracker sheets

½   cup 1% low-fat milk

½   ounce semisweet chocolate, grated

3   cups fat-free vanilla light ice cream

1. Preheat broiler.

2. Place marshmallows on a baking sheet lined with parchment paper. Broil 45 seconds or until puffed and toasted. Cool on pan 2 minutes.

3. Crush 4 graham cracker sheets into a blender. Add milk, 4 toasted marshmallows, chocolate, and ice cream; process until smooth. Pour milk shake into 4 glasses. Top each shake with 1 marshmallow. Serve immediately. Serves 4 (serving size: ⅔ cup)

CALORIES 288; FAT 3g (sat 1g, mono 0.8g, poly 0.7g); PROTEIN 7g; CARB 60g; FIBER 0.7g; CHOL 2mg; IRON 0.8mg; SODIUM 170mg; CALC 162mg

spicy blood orange cooler

Ginger gives this cooler a little kick, and it gets its pretty color from blood orange juice. You can also use regular orange juice. Garnish glasses with a blood orange slice, if desired.

1¾ cups bottled blood orange juice

1¾ cups chopped mango (2 mangos), frozen

1 tablespoon grated peeled fresh ginger

3 tablespoons honey

⅛ teaspoon sea salt

1 cup tangerine-orange flavored sparkling water

1. Combine first 5 ingredients in a blender; process until smooth.

2. Pour mixture into an 8-inch square glass or ceramic baking dish. Cover and freeze 2½ hours, scraping with a fork every 30 minutes until mixture is fluffy.

3. Spoon orange mixture into 4 serving glasses. Top each with ¼ cup sparkling water. Serve immediately. Serves 4 (serving size: 1 cup)

CALORIES 141; FAT 0.3g (sat 0g, mono 0.1g, poly 0g); PROTEIN 1g; CARB 35g; FIBER 1g; CHOL 0mg; IRON 0mg; SODIUM 85mg; CALC 18mg

strawberry milk shake

Add malted milk powder to turn this into a strawberry malt.

- 2   cups vanilla low-fat ice cream
- ¼   cup fat-free milk
- 1   tablespoon sugar
- 1   (16-ounce) container strawberries, hulled
- 6   whole strawberries with green caps (optional)

1. Place first 4 ingredients in a blender, and process 1 minute or until smooth, scraping sides as necessary. Pour into 3 glasses. Garnish each serving with skewered strawberry halves, if desired. Serve immediately. Serves 3 (serving size: 1 cup)

CALORIES 218; FAT 3.1g (sat 1.4g, mono 0.1g, poly 0.2g); PROTEIN 5.7g; CARB 42.2g; FIBER 4.4g; CHOL 7mg; IRON 1mg; SODIUM 70mg; CALC 183mg

skip the dairy

Substitute vanilla-flavored dairy-free frozen dessert for the ice cream, and vanilla soy milk for the fat-free milk.

sweet cherry slush

1   (12-ounce) package frozen pitted dark sweet cherries

¾   cup unsweetened cranberry juice, chilled

¾   cup apple juice, chilled

4   tablespoons honey

1   tablespoon fresh lemon juice

⅛   teaspoon almond extract

15 ice cubes

1. Place all ingredients in a blender; process until slushy. Serves 4 (serving size: 1 cup)

CALORIES 181; FAT 0g (sat 0g, mono 0g, poly 0g); PROTEIN 2g; CARB 47g; FIBER 1g; CHOL 0mg; IRON 0.5mg; SODIUM 3mg; CALC 21mg

check your chill IQ

A small Cherry Limeade at Sonic contains about the same amount of carbohydrates as _____?

A. 1 hot dog (24 grams)
B. 1 hamburger (31 grams)
C. 7 fried chicken drumsticks (42 grams)
D. 1 chicken sandwich (55 grams)

Answer: C. A single Cherry Limeade contains 45 grams of carbohydrates.

watermelon-strawberry slush

Strawberries and watermelon have a natural affinity for each other; together, they deliver vitamin C and lycopene, which are good for your heart. Dress up this slush with watermelon wedges, if desired.

1   (16-ounce) container fresh strawberries

4   cups (1-inch) watermelon cubes

¼   cup honey

2   tablespoons chopped mint

2   tablespoons fresh lime juice

1. Hull the strawberries and place them on a baking sheet. Freeze for 1 hour 20 minutes, or until frozen.

2. Place watermelon in a blender; process until liquefied. Add honey, mint, lime juice, and strawberries; process until smooth. Serves 4 (serving size: 1¼ cups)

CALORIES 148; FAT 0.6g (sat 0g, mono 0.1g, poly 0.3g); PROTEIN 1.9g; CARB 38g; FIBER 3g; CHOL 0mg; IRON 0.9mg; SODIUM 4mg; CALC 33mg

juices & drinks

Use fruits, vegetables, and herbs to create your own juices. Give yourself an energy boost, a dose of vitamins, or a refreshing sip.

asian pear sparkler

Lemongrass, cucumber, and Asian pear add a note of sophistication to this sweet drink. Be sure to put the pear and cucumber in the blender first.

4½ **cups (1-inch) cubed Asian pear (about 3 pears)**

2   **cups (1-inch) cubed peeled cucumber (1 large)**

2   **tablespoons fresh lime juice (about 2 limes)**

1   **(8-inch) stalk peeled fresh lemongrass, chopped**

2   **(12-ounce) bottles sparkling apple drink, chilled**

4   **Asian pear slices (optional)**

1. Place first 4 ingredients in blender; process 1 minute or until blended and almost smooth. Strain mixture through a sieve into a bowl, pressing with the back of a spoon; discard solids. Cover and refrigerate 1 hour or until thoroughly chilled.

2. Pour ½ cup pear mixture into each of 4 glasses; top each serving with ¾ cup sparkling apple drink, and stir gently. Garnish each serving with 1 pear slice, if desired. Serves 4

CALORIES 157; FAT 0.3g (sat 0g, mono 0g, poly 0g); PROTEIN 1.1g; CARB 40.1g; FIBER 4.7g; CHOL 0mg; IRON 0.4mg; SODIUM 8mg; CALC 23mg

blueberry-ginger juice

Ginger aids in digestion and adds a bit of tropical flair to this juice that is loaded with antioxidants.

½ **cup sugar**

½ **cup water**

¼ **cup coarsely chopped peeled fresh ginger**

6 **(2-inch-long) strips lemon rind**

4 **cups blueberries**

2 **teaspoons grated peeled fresh ginger**

2 **(10-ounce) bottles club soda, chilled**

Ice cubes

Lemon rind strips or lemon slices (optional)

1. Combine first 4 ingredients in a medium saucepan. Bring to a boil, stirring until sugar dissolves. Remove from heat; let stand 15 minutes. Place pan in a large ice-filled bowl for 5 minutes or until cold. Pour syrup through a sieve into a pitcher; discard solids.

2. Place half of blueberries and grated ginger in a blender; process 20 seconds or until smooth. Pour blueberry puree through a sieve into pitcher, pressing with the back of a spoon to remove as much juice as possible; discard solids. Stir juice into syrup mixture. Repeat procedure with remaining blueberries and grated ginger. Cover and refrigerate until ready to serve.

3. Gently stir club soda into blueberry mixture. Serve immediately over ice. Garnish with lemon rind strips or slices, if desired. Serves 5 (serving size: about 1 cup)

CALORIES 151; FAT 0.4g (sat 0.1g, mono 0.1g, poly 0.2g); PROTEIN 1g; CARB 38.7g; FIBER 3.2g; CHOL 0mg; IRON 0.4mg; SODIUM 26mg; CALC 17mg

carrot, apple, and ginger refresher

If you'd like this drink to be more tart, use plain instead of vanilla fat-free yogurt. For a garnish, twist a thin slice of carrot on a small skewer.

½ cup 100% carrot juice, chilled

½ cup unsweetened applesauce

½ cup organic vanilla fat-free yogurt

1 teaspoon fresh lemon juice (from 1 lemon)

½ teaspoon grated peeled fresh ginger

1 frozen sliced ripe banana

5 ice cubes (about 2 ounces)

1. Place all ingredients in a blender; process 2 minutes or until smooth. Serve immediately. Serves 2 (serving size: about 1¼ cups)

CALORIES 138; FAT 0.1g (sat 0g, mono 0g, poly 0.1g); PROTEIN 4.3g; CARB 32.7g; FIBER 2.3g; CHOL 2mg; IRON 0.3mg; SODIUM 79mg; CALC 126mg

chamomile-ginger iced tea

Need a caffeine-free alternative to sweet tea? This recipe is flavored with lemon, honey, and ginger.

8 cups water

6 tablespoons honey

2 tablespoons grated peeled fresh ginger

2 tablespoons fresh lemon juice (about 2 lemons)

12 chamomile tea bags

4 (2-inch-long) strips lemon rind

Ice

Lemon wedges (optional)

1. Bring 8 cups water to a boil in a 3-quart saucepan. Remove pan from heat; add honey and next 4 ingredients (through lemon rind). Steep 1 hour and 30 minutes.

2. Pour tea mixture through a sieve into a pitcher; discard solids. Cover and refrigerate until thoroughly chilled. Serve over ice, and garnish with lemon wedges, if desired. Serves 6 (serving size: about 1⅓ cups)

CALORIES 69; FAT 0g (sat 0g, mono 0g, poly 0g); PROTEIN 0.2g; CARB 18.8g; FIBER 0.6g; CHOL 0mg; IRON 0.1mg; SODIUM 1mg; CALC 8mg

cherry sparkler

Here's a version of a cherry limeade that uses real juice instead of syrup. Ginger soda adds a spicy note.

2   **cups bottled black cherry juice**
1   **cup lime-flavored sparkling water**
1   **cup sparkling ginger soda**
2   **tablespoons fresh lime juice (about 2 large limes)**
1   **cup frozen pitted dark sweet cherries**

Thin lime slices (optional)

1. Combine first 4 ingredients in a pitcher. Cover and refrigerate 1 hour or until thoroughly chilled. Add about 2 to 3 frozen cherries to each glass. Pour 1 cup cherry juice mixture over cherries in each glass. Garnish with lime slices, if desired. Serves 4 (serving size: 1 cup sparkler and 4 to 5 cherries)

CALORIES 122; FAT 0g (sat 0g, mono 0g, poly 0g); PROTEIN 1.5g; CARB 31.2g; FIBER 1.3g; CHOL 0mg; IRON 0.1mg; SODIUM 17mg; CALC 6mg

cucumber, apple, and mint cooler

Drink this to boost your daily veggie count: Each serving gives you a half-cup of vegetables, plus a little fruit. Garnish with cucumber slices, if desired.

⅓ cup unsweetened frozen 100% apple juice concentrate, undiluted

¼ cup cold water

1 cup chopped seeded peeled cucumber (about ½ pound)

¼ cup chopped mint

10 ice cubes

1. Place all ingredients in a blender; process 2 minutes or until smooth. Serve immediately. Serves 2 (serving size: 1 cup)

CALORIES 91; FAT 0.4g (sat 0.1g, mono 0g, poly 0.1g); PROTEIN 1g; CARB 21.6g; FIBER 1.4g; CHOL 0mg; IRON 2mg; SODIUM 16mg; CALC 41mg

cucumber agua fresca

Serve this refreshing drink with spicy, grilled foods. Use a vegetable peeler to make the optional cucumber ribbons—simply run the peeler along the cucumber lengthwise.

2   tablespoons sugar

3   tablespoons water

1¾ cups peeled English cucumber slices (about 1 medium cucumber)

¼   cup water

3   tablespoons fresh lime juice (about 2 large limes)

1½ cups crushed ice

2   cups lime-flavored sparkling water, chilled

English cucumber ribbons (optional)

1. Combine sugar and 3 tablespoons water in a small microwave-safe bowl. Microwave at HIGH 2 minutes or until mixture boils, stirring every 1 minute. Cool.

2. Place cucumber slices and ¼ cup water in a blender; process until smooth. Strain mixture through a cheesecloth-lined sieve into a bowl to measure 1 cup liquid; discard solids. Combine cucumber liquid and sugar syrup in a small pitcher. Cover and refrigerate 1 hour or until thoroughly chilled; stir in lime juice.

3. Place ¾ cup crushed ice in each of 2 glasses. Pour ½ cup cucumber mixture into each glass. Add 1 cup sparkling water to each glass. Garnish with cucumber ribbons, if desired. Serves 2

CALORIES 44; FAT 0.1g (sat 0g, mono 0g, poly 0g); PROTEIN 0.5g; CARB 11.1g; FIBER 0.5g; CHOL 0mg; IRON 0.2mg; SODIUM 32mg; CALC 12mg

hibiscus–ginger sparkler

Purchase commercially made ginger syrup at specialty grocery stores.

2 cups water

¼ cup loose hibiscus tea

¼ cup sugar

½ cup pomegranate juice

2 tablespoons ginger syrup

Ice cubes

2 cups lime-flavored sparkling water, chilled

Lime slices (optional)

1. Bring 2 cups water to a boil in a medium saucepan. Stir in tea; cover and steep 5 minutes.

2. Place sugar in a pitcher. Pour warm tea through a sieve over sugar, stirring until sugar dissolves. Discard tea leaves. Cool completely.

3. Stir pomegranate juice and ginger syrup into tea mixture; cover and refrigerate until thoroughly chilled.

4. Fill each of 4 glasses with ice. Pour ⅔ cup tea mixture over ice in each glass; add ½ cup sparkling water to each glass. Garnish with lime slices, if desired. Serves 4

CALORIES 86; FAT 0g (sat 0g, mono 0g, poly 0g); PROTEIN 0.1g; CARB 22g; FIBER 0g; CHOL 0mg; IRON 0.1mg; SODIUM 26mg; CALC 5mg

honeydew spritzer

Honeydew melon, naturally low in calories, is a good source of vitamin C and potassium. A touch of sea salt boosts the melon's flavor.

1   cup unsweetened white grape juice, chilled

3   tablespoons fresh lime juice (about 2 large limes)

1   tablespoon honey

⅛   teaspoon coarse sea salt

2   cups (1-inch) cubed honeydew melon, frozen

Ice

1⅓ cups club soda, chilled

Fresh lime slices (optional)

1. Place first 4 ingredients in a blender; process until smooth. Remove center piece of blender lid; secure blender lid on blender. With blender on, drop melon cubes, 1 to 2 at a time, through lid. Process until smooth.

2. Fill 4 glasses with ice. Pour ¾ cup honeydew mixture over ice in each glass; add ⅓ cup club soda to each glass. Garnish with lime slices, if desired. Serves 4

CALORIES 89; FAT 0.1g (sat 0g, mono 0g, poly 0.1g); PROTEIN 0.5g; CARB 22.8g; FIBER 0.7g; CHOL 0mg; IRON 0.2mg; SODIUM 107mg; CALC 11mg

mango punch

Don't judge a mango by its color—it isn't a good sign of ripeness. Instead, choose a mango that gives slightly when you gently squeeze it.

1 cup orange juice

4 cups (1-inch) cubed mango (about 2 large mangos)

1 cup sliced strawberries

3 tablespoons fresh lime juice (about 2 large limes)

4 cups sparkling ginger or lime soda

Ice

1. Place half of first 4 ingredients in a blender; process until smooth. Pour into a pitcher. Repeat with remaining half of ingredients. Chill until ready to serve. Gently stir in soda. Serve over ice. Serves 8 (serving size: 1 cup)

CALORIES 113; FAT 0.5g (sat 0.1g, mono 0.1g, poly 0.1g); PROTEIN 1.1g; CARB 27.7g; FIBER 1.8g; CHOL 0mg; IRON 0.3mg; SODIUM 3mg; CALC 17mg

to your health

Blend this punch when your immune system needs a boost: oranges, mangos, and strawberries are all loaded with vitamin C. (A cup of mango alone gives you your daily dose.)

milk with hot chocolate ice cubes

5 cups 2% reduced-fat milk, divided

½ cup water

¼ cup sugar

¼ cup unsweetened cocoa

1 teaspoon vanilla extract

2 ounces dark chocolate, finely chopped

1. Bring 1 cup milk and ½ cup water to a boil in a medium saucepan. Reduce heat to medium. Combine sugar and cocoa, stirring with a whisk. Add sugar mixture to hot milk mixture, stirring with a whisk until blended. Bring to a simmer; simmer 5 minutes, stirring frequently. Remove pan from heat; add vanilla and chocolate, stirring with a whisk until chocolate melts. Pour milk mixture into 2 ice cube trays. Cool 30 minutes. Freeze 4 hours or until firm.

2. Place 4 chocolate ice cubes in each of 6 glasses; add ⅔ cup milk to each glass. Serves 6 (serving size: 1 drink)

CALORIES 196; FAT 7.5g (sat 4.6g, mono 2.2g, poly 0.3g); PROTEIN 7.9g; CARB 26.1g; FIBER 1.8g; CHOL 17mg; IRON 1mg; SODIUM 99mg; CALC 254mg

mint limeade

Try serving this as a refreshing cooler with spicy Asian food.

6   cups water, divided

1¾ cups sugar

⅓   cup coarsely chopped mint

1   cup fresh lime juice (about 12 limes)

Ice

10 mint sprigs (optional)

10 lime slices (optional)

1. Combine 2 cups water, sugar, and chopped mint in a small saucepan; bring to a boil. Cook until sugar dissolves, stirring frequently. Remove from heat; let stand 10 minutes. Strain through a sieve into a bowl; discard solids.

2. Combine 4 cups water, sugar syrup, and lime juice in a large pitcher, stirring well. Serve over ice; garnish with mint sprigs and lime slices, if desired. Serves 10 (serving size: about ¾ cup)

CALORIES 143; FAT 0g (sat 0g, mono 0g, poly 0g); PROTEIN 0.1g; CARB 37.4g; FIBER 0.2g; CHOL 0mg; IRON 0.1mg; SODIUM 1mg; CALC 6mg

orange-carrot refresher

Ginger paste and mint paste are available in resealable tubes in the produce section of the grocery store. If you can't find the pastes, substitute 1 tablespoon grated ginger and 10 mint leaves. Combine the first 6 ingredients in a blender and process until smooth, then pour the mixture into a pitcher and stir in the carrot juice.

2   cups fresh orange juice (about 4 oranges)

2   tablespoons fresh lime juice (about 2 large limes)

1   tablespoon brown sugar

1   tablespoon refrigerated ginger paste

1   teaspoon refrigerated mint paste

Dash of salt

2   cups 100% carrot juice, chilled

Ice cubes

Mint sprigs (optional)

1. Place first 6 ingredients in a large pitcher; stir with a whisk. Add carrot juice; stir until blended. Serve over ice. Garnish with mint sprigs, if desired. Serves 5 (serving size: 1 cup)

CALORIES 86; FAT 0.2g (sat 0g, mono 0g, poly 0g); PROTEIN 1.6g; CARB 19.4g; FIBER 0.3g; CHOL 0mg; IRON 0.4mg; SODIUM 92mg; CALC 31mg

check your chill IQ

A small Orange Julius Original contains about the same amount of sugar as _____?

    A. 1 serving Kellogg's Frosted Flakes cereal (11 grams)
    B. 1 (12-oz.) can lemon-lime soda (37 grams)
    C. 1 (8-oz.) orange drink (28 grams)
    D. 4 (3.25-oz.) containers chocolate pudding (56 grams)

Answer: D. A small Orange Julius Original contains 59 grams of sugar.

peach lemonade

Use ripe, juicy summer peaches—their sweet flavor will balance the tart lemon.

4 **cups water**

2 **cups coarsely chopped peaches**

¾ **cup sugar**

1 **cup fresh lemon juice (about 6 lemons)**

4 **cups ice**

1 **peach, pitted and cut into 8 wedges**

Lemon slices (optional)

1. Combine first 3 ingredients in a medium saucepan over medium-high heat. Bring to a boil; reduce heat, and simmer 3 minutes. Place peach mixture in a blender; let stand 20 minutes. Remove center piece of blender lid (to allow steam to escape); secure blender lid on blender. Place a clean towel over opening in blender lid (to avoid splatters). Blend until smooth. Pour into a large bowl. Refrigerate at least 3 hours.

2. Press peach mixture through a sieve over a bowl, reserving liquid; discard solids. Stir in lemon juice. Place ½ cup ice in each of 8 glasses. Pour about ⅔ cup lemonade into each glass; garnish each glass with 1 peach wedge and a lemon slice, if desired. Serves 8

CALORIES 102; FAT 0.2g (sat 0g, mono 0g, poly 0.1g); PROTEIN 0.6g; CARB 26.5g; FIBER 0.9g; CHOL 0mg; IRON 0.2mg; SODIUM 0mg; CALC 5mg

peachy grape cooler

Frozen peaches do double duty in this frosty drink: Not only do they add flavor, they keep the drink cold without diluting it as ice would.

1½ cups 100% white grape juice, chilled

1½ cups peach juice, chilled

2 (12-ounce) bottles sparkling peach juice beverage, chilled

1 cup frozen peach slices

1. Combine first 3 ingredients in a pitcher. Gently stir in peach slices. Serve immediately. Serves 7 (serving size: 1 cup)

CALORIES 91; FAT 0.1g (sat 0g, mono 0g, poly 0g); PROTEIN 0.4g; CARB 22.9g; FIBER 0.3g; CHOL 0mg; IRON 0.2mg; SODIUM 9mg; CALC 9mg

pear-apple-cranberry punch

This punch is full of fall flavors that are sweetened with a bit of maple syrup and brightened with citrus.

3   cups pear nectar

2   cups apple juice, chilled

2   cups unsweetened cranberry juice, chilled

2   tablespoons maple syrup

1   tablespoon fresh lime juice (about 1 lime)

1   tablespoon fresh lemon juice (about 1 lemon)

5   (⅛-inch-thick) slices peeled fresh ginger

1   cup club soda

Apple slices (optional)

Pear slices (optional)

Lime slices (optional)

Lemon slices (optional)

1. Combine first 7 ingredients in a large bowl. Cover and chill at least 3 hours or up to 8 hours; discard ginger.

2. Pour juice mixture into a punch bowl. Stir in club soda. Garnish with apple, pear, lime, and lemon slices, if desired. Serve immediately. Serves 8 (serving size: about 1 cup)

CALORIES 129; FAT 0.2g (sat 0g, mono 0g, poly 0.1g); PROTEIN 0.5g; CARB 33.4g; FIBER 0.8g; CHOL 0mg; IRON 0.5mg; SODIUM 15mg; CALC 22mg

pineapple agua fresca

Agua fresca, "fresh water," is a non-alcoholic drink made with fresh fruit that is popular in Mexico. It's a delicious way to cool down.

3 cups cubed fresh pineapple

2 cups cold water

1 tablespoon sugar

1 tablespoon fresh lime juice

1 tablespoon chopped fresh mint

Ice

Fresh pineapple wedges (optional)

1. Combine first 4 ingredients in a blender; process 1 minute or until smooth.

2. Strain mixture through a sieve into a pitcher; discard solids. Stir in mint. Cover and chill until ready to serve. Serve over ice, and, if desired, garnish with pineapple wedges. Serves 4 (serving size: 1 cup)

CALORIES 75; FAT 0.2g (sat 0g, mono 0g, poly 0.1g); PROTEIN 0.7g; CARB 19.8g; FIBER 1.8g; CHOL 0mg; IRON 0.4mg; SODIUM 1mg; CALC 18mg

pink grapefruit fizz

This invigorating drink is for grownups who prefer tart to sweet. Unlike nutrition-empty sodas, this one has plenty of vitamin C. If you like, serve it in a salt-rimmed glass with a sprig of rosemary.

1 cup fresh pink grapefruit juice (about 3 grapefruits)

1 tablespoon sugar

2 tablespoons pomegranate juice

Ice cubes

1 cup club soda, chilled

Grapefruit wedges (optional)

1. Combine first 3 ingredients in a 2-cup glass measure, stirring until sugar dissolves. Fill 2 glasses with ice. Pour juice mixture and club soda evenly over ice. Garnish with grapefruit wedges, if desired. Serve immediately. Serves 2 (serving size: 1 cup)

CALORIES 81; FAT 0.1g (sat 0g, mono 0g, poly 0g); PROTEIN 0.7g; CARB 19.9g; FIBER 0g; CHOL 0mg; IRON 0.3mg; SODIUM 28mg; CALC 20mg

plum-thyme iced tea

You can use pluots in place of the plums when they're in season from May through late summer.

4¾ cups water, divided

6 regular-sized tea bags

½ cup sugar

2½ cups chopped pitted red plums (about 3 plums)

3 thyme sprigs

Ice

1 red plum, thinly sliced (optional)

Lemon slices (optional)

1. Bring 4 cups water to a boil in a medium saucepan. Remove pan from heat, and add tea bags. Cover and steep 5 minutes. Remove and discard tea bags. Cool tea completely in pan.

2. Combine ¾ cup water, sugar, chopped plums, and thyme in a medium saucepan. Bring to a boil, stirring until sugar melts. Reduce heat, and simmer, uncovered, 15 minutes or until plums are very tender and have lost their shape. Strain plum mixture through a sieve into tea, pressing with the back of a spoon to extract juice. Discard solids. Stir tea mixture; cover and refrigerate until thoroughly chilled.

3. Serve tea over ice. Garnish with plum and lemon slices, if desired. Serves 4 (serving size: about 1 cup)

CALORIES 124; FAT 0g (sat 0g, mono 0g, poly 0g); PROTEIN 0.4g; CARB 32.4g; FIBER 0.8g; CHOL 0mg; IRON 0.2mg; SODIUM 0mg; CALC 1mg

pomegranate–apple shrub

Shrubs are old-time thirst quenchers made with a bit of vinegar for tang (and they're coming back, thanks to new interest in drinking vinegars). Originally, shrubs were prepared with lots of sugar, but this one is made healthier with only the natural sugars from the fruit.

1¼ **cups pomegranate juice**   2 **tablespoons cider vinegar**

1¼ **cups unsweetened apple cider**   **Ice**

1. Combine first 3 ingredients in a pitcher. Cover and refrigerate 1 hour or until thoroughly chilled.

2. Fill 3 glasses with ice; pour shrub over ice. Serve immediately. Serves 3 (serving size: about 1 cup)

CALORIES 117; FAT 0g (sat 0g, mono 0g, poly 0g); PROTEIN 0.8g; CARB 29.3g; FIBER 0g; CHOL 0mg; IRON 0.2mg; SODIUM 15mg; CALC 17mg

raspberry-peach lemonade

Kick up classic raspberry lemonade: Peach and ginger add a sweet-spicy twist.

- 4 cups water
- 1 cup coarsely chopped peeled peach (about 1 large peach)
- ¾ cup sugar
- 1 tablespoon grated peeled fresh ginger
- 1 (6-ounce) container raspberries
- 1 cup fresh lemon juice (about 6 large lemons)

Ice

1. Place first 5 ingredients in a medium saucepan. Bring to a boil; reduce heat, and simmer, uncovered, 3 minutes. Remove from heat; cool slightly.

2. Strain mixture through a sieve into a bowl, reserving liquid and solids. Place solids in a blender; process until smooth.

3. Combine pureed mixture and liquid. Stir in lemon juice. Cover and refrigerate 1 hour or until thoroughly chilled. Serve over ice. Serves 6 (serving size: 1 cup)

CALORIES 133; FAT 0.3g (sat 0g, mono 0g, poly 0.1g); PROTEIN 0.8g; CARB 35g; FIBER 2.4g; CHOL 0mg; IRON 0.3mg; SODIUM 1mg; CALC 12mg

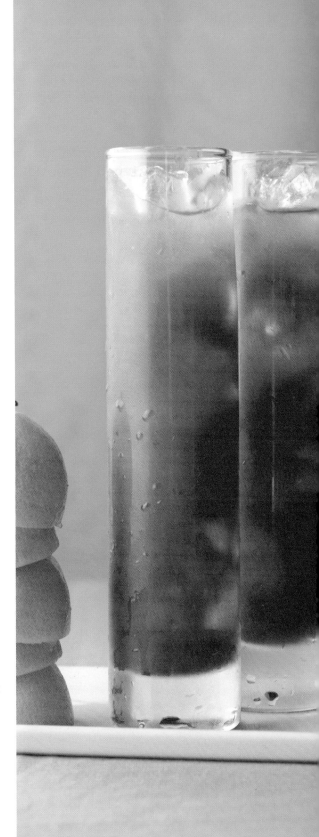

real ginger ale

Making your own ginger ale is easier than you might think, and it captures all the spicy warmth ginger lovers enjoy. One sip, and you'll be spoiled.

2½ cups water

1   cup chopped peeled fresh ginger

⅓   cup chopped crystallized ginger

½   cup honey

4½ cups seltzer water, chilled

Ice

1. Combine first 3 ingredients in a 2-quart saucepan. Bring to a boil. Cover, reduce heat, and simmer 30 minutes. Uncover; increase heat to medium, and cook 10 minutes or until ginger is very tender. Remove pan from heat; cover and let stand 30 minutes.

2. Strain ginger mixture through a sieve into a bowl. Discard solids. Stir in honey until blended. Cover and refrigerate 2 hours or until thoroughly chilled.

3. Place 4 tablespoons ginger syrup in each of 6 chilled glasses. Stir ¾ cup seltzer into each glass. Add ice, and serve immediately. Serves 6 (serving size: about 1 cup)

CALORIES 136; FAT 0.1g (sat 0g, mono 0g, poly 0g); PROTEIN 0.5g; CARB 35.4g; FIBER 0.3g; CHOL 0mg; IRON 0.6mg; SODIUM 7mg; CALC 19mg

ruby sipper

Beets are nutritional powerhouses, giving you vitamin C, iron, potassium, and fiber. Choose beets with fresh-looking green tops, and wear gloves or use a kitchen towel when handling them to prevent your fingers from getting stained.

- 1¼ cups pitted dark sweet cherries
- 1¼ cups fresh pineapple chunks
- 1 cup light coconut milk
- ¼ cup chopped peeled fresh beets
- 1 tablespoon fresh lime juice (about 1 large lime)
- 3 tablespoons honey

Unpeeled pineapple wedges (optional)

1. Place all ingredients in a blender; process until smooth. Strain mixture through a sieve; discard solids. Pour into glasses. Garnish with pineapple wedges, if desired. Serve immediately. Serves 4 (serving size: ⅔ cup)

CALORIES 116; FAT 0.9g (sat 0.6g, mono 0g, poly 0.1g); PROTEIN 1.2g; CARB 28.7g; FIBER 2g; CHOL 0mg; IRON 0.4mg; SODIUM 10mg; CALC 16mg

star fruit quencher

The star fruit, or carambola, is the "star" of this beverage and tastes like a blend of apple, pear, and citrus fruits. The entire fruit is edible. Here, it is pureed and then strained to create a delicious, fragrant juice.

½ cup pineapple juice

4 carambolas (star fruit); (about 1¼ pounds), cut into
   ½-inch slices

3 tablespoons ginger syrup

1 tablespoon fresh lemon juice (about 1 lemon)

2 cups crushed ice

½ cup lemon-lime-flavored sparkling water, chilled

Carambola slices (optional)

1. Place pineapple juice and carambola slices in a blender; process until smooth. Pour mixture through a sieve into a pitcher to measure 2 cups. Discard solids. Stir in ginger syrup and lemon juice. Cover and refrigerate 45 minutes or until thoroughly chilled.

2. Fill each of 2 glasses with 1 cup crushed ice. Pour star fruit mixture over ice. Add ¼ cup sparkling water to each glass. Garnish with carambola slices, if desired. Serves 2 (serving size: 1 drink)

CALORIES 183; FAT 1g (sat 0.1g, mono 0.1g, poly 0.6g); PROTEIN 3.2g; CARB 42.8g; FIBER 8g; CHOL 0mg; IRON 0.4mg; SODIUM 18mg; CALC 17mg

strawberry–basil limeade

Buy strawberries at their seasonal peak and taste them—if they're very sweet, you may want to adjust the amount of sugar syrup you use to make this limeade.

¾ **cup sugar**

¾ **cup water**

¼ **cup basil leaves**

1½ **cups strawberries, quartered**

1 **cup fresh lime juice (about 12 limes)**

5 **cups lime-flavored sparkling water, chilled**

Ice cubes

Basil leaves (optional)

1. Combine first 3 ingredients in a small saucepan. Bring to a boil over medium-high heat, stirring constantly until sugar dissolves. Remove from heat, and cool 30 minutes or until room temperature.

2. Strain basil mixture through a sieve into a large pitcher, discarding basil. Place strawberries and lime juice in a blender; process until smooth. Add strawberry mixture to basil mixture. Gently stir in sparkling water. Serve immediately over ice. Garnish with basil leaves, if desired. Serves 8 (serving size: 1 cup)

CALORIES 91; FAT 0.1g (sat 0g, mono 0g, poly 0.1g); PROTEIN 0.4g; CARB 23.9g; FIBER 0.8g; CHOL 0mg; IRON 0.2mg; SODIUM 29mg; CALC 12mg

strawberry-kiwi juice

Make this when you want a large dose of vitamin C: Kiwifruit contain more of the antioxidant than oranges, and strawberries are a good source of C, too. Kiwifruit has also been shown to support eye health.

4 cups strawberry halves

1 cup quartered peeled kiwifruit (about 2 kiwifruit)

1 cup water

2 tablespoons fresh lime juice (about 2 limes)

3 tablespoons honey

Ice (optional)

1. Place all ingredients in a blender; process until smooth. Strain mixture through a sieve into a pitcher; discard solids. Cover and refrigerate 30 minutes or until thoroughly chilled. Serve over ice, if desired. Serves 4 (serving size: about 1 cup)

CALORIES 119; FAT 0.6g (sat 0g, mono 0.1g, poly 0.3g); PROTEIN 1.5g; CARB 30.1g; FIBER 4.1g; CHOL 0mg; IRON 0.8mg; SODIUM 3mg; CALC 38mg

tangerine spiced tea punch

Subtly spiced, this tea-based citrus drink is a fragrant cooling infusion to make you dream of exotic afternoons. Choose black tea flavored with orange and spices as the base.

¾ cup water

2 tablespoons sugar

2 black tea bags flavored with orange and spices

3 large tangerines (about 1¼ pounds)

Ice

1 cup ginger ale

1. Combine ¾ cup water and sugar in a small saucepan. Bring to a boil; remove from heat. Add tea bags, and steep 10 minutes. Remove and discard tea bags.

2. While tea steeps, squeeze juice from tangerines to measure 1 cup. Stir juice into tea.

3. Fill 2 glasses with ice.

4. Stir ginger ale into tea mixture. Pour over ice. Serves 2 (serving size: about 1¼ cups)

CALORIES 186; FAT 0.6g (sat 0.1g, mono 0.1g, poly 0.1g); PROTEIN 1.5g; CARB 47.3g; FIBER 3.2g; CHOL 0mg; IRON 0.5mg; SODIUM 12mg; CALC 70mg

vanilla-pomegranate italian soda

Pomegranate juice is chock-full of antioxidants, but it can be very tart. Vanilla syrup mellows the tartness, creating a sophisticated soda.

¼   cup sugar

¼   cup water

¼   teaspoon vanilla extract

3   cups seltzer, chilled

1   cup pomegranate juice, chilled

Ice

1. Combine sugar and ¼ cup water in a small saucepan. Bring to a boil, stirring constantly until sugar dissolves. Remove from heat; stir in vanilla. Cool 30 minutes or until room temperature.

2. Combine cooled vanilla syrup, seltzer, and pomegranate juice in a pitcher. Fill each of 4 glasses with ice; divide soda among glasses. Serves 4 (serving size: about 1 cup)

CALORIES 85; FAT 0g (sat 0g, mono 0g, poly 0g); PROTEIN 0.3g; CARB 21.4g; FIBER 0g; CHOL 0mg; IRON 0mg; SODIUM 45mg; CALC 19mg

tasty twist

Use this recipe as inspiration to make your own Italian sodas: Swap the pomegranate juice for another intense juice, like cherry or blueberry. You can also change the syrup flavor with extracts or herbs.

watermelon mojito smash

½ cup water

¼ cup sugar

2 (5-inch) mint sprigs

2 cups cubed seeded watermelon

2 tablespoons fresh lime juice (about 2 large limes)

Ice cubes

1 cup lime-flavored sparkling water, chilled

Mint sprigs (optional)

Lime slices (optional)

1. Combine ½ cup water and sugar in a small saucepan. Bring to a boil. Cook, uncovered, 1 minute or until sugar dissolves. Remove from heat and stir in 2 (5-inch) mint sprigs. Cover and steep 15 minutes. Remove and discard mint. Cool mint syrup completely.

2. Place watermelon in a blender; process until smooth. Strain watermelon mixture through a sieve into a bowl; discard solids. Stir in mint syrup and lime juice.

3. Fill each of 2 glasses with ice cubes. Pour ¾ cup watermelon mixture and ½ cup sparkling water over ice in each glass. Garnish with additional mint sprigs and lime slices, if desired. Serves 2 (serving size: 1¼ cups)

CALORIES 147; FAT 0.2g (sat 0g, mono 0.1g, poly 0.1g); PROTEIN 1g; CARB 38g; FIBER 0.7g; CHOL 0mg; IRON 0.4mg; SODIUM 25mg; CALC 13mg

ices

You may have fallen in love with sweet ices as a kid. Rekindle your love affair with ices for a light dessert or a between-courses palate refresher.

apricot ice with roasted almonds

For a special presentation, place a few slices of fresh apricot in the bottom of a small serving dish, and top with this delicious ice. The ice will keep in the freezer up to three days. Garnish with curls of lemon rind.

2   tablespoons sugar

3   tablespoons fresh lemon juice (about 2 large lemons)

⅛   teaspoon salt

⅛   teaspoon almond extract

1   (11.3-ounce) can apricot nectar

¼   cup finely chopped honey-roasted almonds

1. Combine first 5 ingredients in an 8-inch glass or ceramic baking dish, stirring 1 minute or until sugar dissolves. Cover and freeze 45 minutes.

2. Scrape nectar mixture with a fork every 45 minutes until frozen (about 3 hours).

3. Remove nectar mixture from freezer; scrape entire mixture with a fork until fluffy. Scoop into serving bowls, and sprinkle with almonds. Serve immediately. Serves 4 (serving size: ½ cup ice and 1 tablespoon almonds)

CALORIES 114; FAT 3.5g (sat 0g, mono 2.8g, poly 0.6g); PROTEIN 1.5g; CARB 19.4g; FIBER 0.5g; CHOL 0mg; IRON 2mg; SODIUM 159mg; CALC 1mg

cherry-almond granita

Almonds and cherries are a classic pair; here, they make a stunning dessert. If you find dark sweet cherries in season, use them in place of the frozen cherries.

2   cups water

⅔   cup sugar

1   pound frozen dark sweet cherries, thawed

¾   teaspoon almond extract

¼   cup fresh lemon juice (about 2 large lemons)

½   cup sliced almonds, toasted

1. Combine first 3 ingredients in a medium saucepan. Bring to a simmer over medium-high heat. Reduce heat to medium and simmer 12 minutes or until cherries are tender. Remove pan from heat; stir in almond extract. Transfer cherry mixture to a bowl. Cool 10 minutes.

2. Place cherry mixture in a blender; add lemon juice, and process until smooth. Pour mixture through a sieve into a bowl, pressing with the back of a spoon to extract juice. Discard solids. Set bowl in a large ice-filled bowl until cold, stirring occasionally.

3. Pour mixture into a 13 x 9–inch glass or ceramic baking dish. Cover and freeze until partially frozen (about 1 hour). Scrape with a fork, crushing any lumps. Freeze, scraping with a fork every hour, an additional 3 hours and 30 minutes or until completely frozen.

4. Spoon granita into bowls; top evenly with almonds. Serves 16 (serving size: ½ cup granita and 1½ teaspoons almonds)

CALORIES 75; FAT 1.4g (sat 0.1g, mono 0.9g, poly 0.4g); PROTEIN 1g; CARB 15.6g; FIBER 0.6g; CHOL 0mg; IRON 0.2mg; SODIUM 0mg; CALC 12mg

cranberry ice

A combination of juices makes this tart ice easy to prepare.

2 cups 100% cranberry juice

⅓ cup sugar

¼ cup fresh lemon juice (about
    2 large lemons)

¼ cup sparkling water

1. Combine cranberry juice and sugar in a medium saucepan. Cook over medium heat 3 minutes or just until sugar dissolves, stirring once. Place pan in a large ice-filled bowl; cool completely, stirring occasionally.

2. Stir in lemon juice and sparkling water. Pour mixture into a 13 x 9–inch glass or ceramic baking dish. Cover and freeze until firm (about 2 hours). Remove mixture from freezer; scrape entire mixture with a fork until fluffy. Serves 7 (serving size: ½ cup)

CALORIES 71; FAT 0g (sat 0g, mono 0g, poly 0g); PROTEIN 0g; CARB 17.8g; FIBER 0g; CHOL 0mg; IRON 0mg; SODIUM 5mg; CALC 13mg

cranberry-jalapeño granita

Finish off the evening with a spicy-sweet iced dessert featuring cranberry juice, mint, and jalapeño pepper. The complex flavors make this an adult favorite that can be enjoyed year-round. Use low-calorie cranberry juice cocktail to lower the calories and sugar.

2 cups cranberry juice cocktail

⅓ cup sugar

4 (5-inch) mint sprigs (about ½ ounce)

1 jalapeño pepper, sliced

2 tablespoons fresh lime juice (about 2 limes)

1. Combine first 4 ingredients in a small saucepan; bring to a boil. Cover and remove from heat; let stand 15 minutes. Strain cranberry mixture through a fine sieve into an 11 x 7–inch glass or ceramic baking dish; discard solids. Cool to room temperature; stir in lime juice. Cover and freeze about 45 minutes. Scrape cranberry mixture every 45 minutes until completely frozen (about 3 hours). Remove mixture from freezer; scrape entire mixture with a fork until fluffy. Serves 4 (serving size: ½ cup)

CALORIES 135; FAT 0.1 (sat 0g, mono 0g, poly 0.1g); PROTEIN 0.1g; CARB 34.5g; FIBER 0.1g; CHOL 0mg; IRON 0.3mg; SODIUM 3mg; CALC 7mg

cucumber-lime granita

Use English cucumbers for fast prep: They have no seeds to remove, and their thinner skin is edible and not bitter.

1 cup water

¾ cup sugar

1 tablespoon grated lime rind (from 2 limes)

½ cup fresh lime juice (about 7 large limes)

¼ teaspoon salt

3 mint sprigs

1 pound chopped English cucumber

1. Combine first 5 ingredients in a small saucepan over medium heat; bring to a boil. Cook 1 minute; remove from heat. Add mint; let stand 10 minutes. Discard mint. Place juice mixture and cucumber in a blender; process until smooth. Cool completely. Pour mixture into an 11 x 7-inch glass or ceramic baking dish.

2. Cover and freeze 45 minutes; scrape with a fork. Freeze. Scrape mixture every 45 minutes until completely frozen (about 3 hours total). Remove from freezer; scrape entire mixture with a fork until fluffy. Serves 6 (serving size: about ½ cup)

CALORIES 112; FAT 0g (sat 0g, mono 0g, poly 0g); PROTEIN 1g; CARB 28.9g; FIBER 1.1g; CHOL 0mg; IRON 0mg; SODIUM 99mg; CALC 5mg

double berry sorbet

You can replace either the raspberries or the blackberries with other fresh, in-season berries if you like. Garnish with fresh berries, if desired.

1¼ **cups water**

½ **cup sugar**

1 **tablespoon fresh lemon juice (about 1 lemon)**

1 **(6-ounce) container raspberries (about 1¼ cups)**

1 **(6-ounce) container blackberries (about 1¼ cups)**

1. Combine all ingredients in a blender; process 30 seconds or until smooth. Press mixture through a fine sieve over a large bowl, reserving liquid; discard solids.

2. Pour berry mixture into the freezer can of an ice-cream freezer; freeze according to manufacturer's instructions. Spoon berry mixture into a freezer-safe container; cover and freeze 2 hours or until firm. Serves 6 (serving size: ½ cup)

CALORIES 92; FAT 0.3g (sat 0g, mono 0g, poly 0.2g); PROTEIN 0.7g; CARB 23g; FIBER 3.2g; CHOL 0mg; IRON 0.4mg; SODIUM 1mg; CALC 16mg

espresso ice

Home-brewed espresso would work just as well in this recipe. You can dress up the finished ice with whipped topping and tri-colored chocolate-covered espresso beans.

1½ **cups boiling water**

¼ **cup packed brown sugar**

1 **tablespoon instant espresso granules**

¼ **cup frozen whipped topping, thawed (optional)**

Chocolate-covered espresso beans (optional)

1. Combine first 3 ingredients in an 8-inch square glass or ceramic baking dish, stirring until sugar and espresso dissolve.

2. Cover and freeze until partially frozen (about 1 hour). Scrape mixture with a fork, crushing any lumps. Freeze an additional 1 hour and 35 minutes or until completely frozen, scraping entire mixture with a fork every 30 minutes.

3. Scoop mixture into espresso cups or small glasses, and, if desired, top with whipped topping and chocolate-covered espresso beans. Serves 4 (serving size: about ½ cup)

CALORIES 53; FAT 0g (sat 0g, mono 0g, poly 0g); PROTEIN 0g; CARB 13.6g; FIBER 0g; CHOL 0mg; IRON 0mg; SODIUM 5mg; CALC 11mg

check your chill IQ

A large Iced Mocha Swirl Latte with milk at Dunkin' Donuts contains the same amount of calories as _____?

   A. 2 chocolate sandwich cookies (107 calories)
   B. 3 ginger snaps (90 calories)
   C. 6 chewy chocolate chip cookies (420 calories)
   D. 1 cup vanilla ice cream (273 calories)

Answer: C. The Mocha Swirl Latte at Dunkin' Donuts sets you back 460 calories.

fresh orange sorbet

To get fresh juice for this sorbet, you'll need about ten medium-sized oranges and three medium-sized lemons.

2½ cups water

1   cup sugar

Orange rind strips from 2 oranges

2⅔ cups fresh orange juice (about 10 oranges)

⅓   cup fresh lemon juice (about 3 lemons)

Orange rind curls (optional)

1. Combine 2½ cups water and sugar in a small saucepan, and bring mixture to a boil. Add orange rind strips; reduce heat, and simmer 5 minutes. Remove and discard orange rind strips. Remove liquid from heat, and cool completely. Stir in orange juice and lemon juice.

2. Pour mixture into the freezer can of a 4-quart ice-cream freezer. Freeze according to manufacturer's instructions. Pack freezer with additional ice and rock salt; let mixture stand in freezer 1 hour before serving.

3. Scoop sorbet into bowls. Garnish with orange rind curls, if desired. Serve immediately. Serves 8 (serving size: ¾ cup)

CALORIES 137; FAT 0.2g (sat 0g, mono 0g, poly 0g); PROTEIN 1g; CARB 34g; FIBER 0.2g; CHOL 0mg; IRON 0mg; SODIUM 1mg; CALC 10mg

grape granita

Our grape granita has soft ice crystals that melt in your mouth, leaving a hint of orange and spice lingering on your tongue.

1   cup unsweetened grape juice
2   tablespoons sugar
2   (4 x 1–inch) orange rind strips
½   (3-inch) cinnamon stick
3½ cups seedless red grapes

1. Place first 4 ingredients in a small saucepan. Cook over medium heat 3 minutes, stirring until sugar dissolves. Remove pan from heat. Cover and let stand 1 hour. Discard rind and cinnamon.

2. Combine juice mixture and grapes in a blender; process until almost smooth. Pour mixture through a fine sieve into a bowl; discard solids.

3. Pour grape mixture into an 8-inch square glass or ceramic baking dish; skim off any foam. Cover and freeze until partially frozen (about 1 hour). Scrape with a fork, crushing any lumps. Freeze 1 hour or until completely frozen; scrape entire mixture with a fork until fluffy. Scoop into glasses, and serve immediately. Serves 6 (serving size: ½ cup)

CALORIES 104; FAT 0.2g (sat 0.1g, mono 0g, poly 0.1g); PROTEIN 0.8g; CARB 26.9g; FIBER 1.2g; CHOL 0mg; IRON 1.6mg; SODIUM 4mg; CALC 15mg

green tea granita

Any flavor of tea will work in this recipe. Brew it stronger or weaker according to your preference. Garnish this delicate dessert with wafer-thin slices of lemon.

3   cups boiling water

4   regular-sized green tea bags

1   (2-inch) piece peeled fresh ginger, quartered

½   cup honey

3   tablespoons fresh lemon juice (about 2 lemons)

1. Pour 3 cups boiling water over tea bags and ginger in a medium bowl. Cover and let stand 5 minutes. Add honey and lemon juice; stir to combine. Strain tea mixture through a sieve into a bowl; discard solids. Cool completely. Pour mixture into an 8-inch square glass or ceramic baking dish. Cover and freeze 8 hours or until firm.

2. Remove tea mixture from freezer; scrape entire mixture with a fork until fluffy. Serves 6 (serving size: about ½ cup)

CALORIES 88; FAT 0g (sat 0g, mono 0g, poly 0g); PROTEIN 0.1g; CARB 23.9g; FIBER 0.1g; CHOL 0mg; IRON 0mg; SODIUM 1mg; CALC 2mg

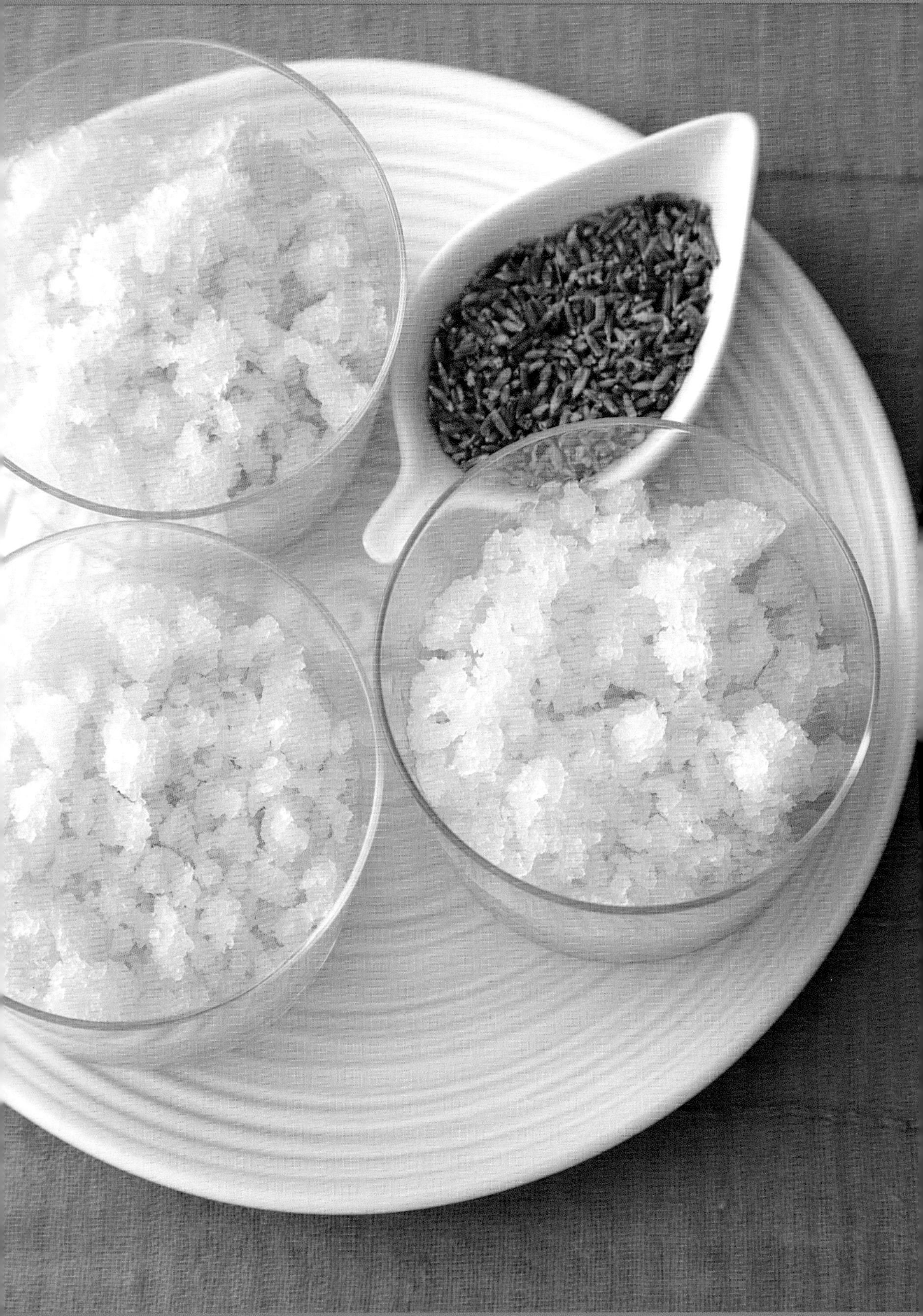

lavender-and-lemon ice

Lychee is a small fruit popular in China, with creamy white flesh and a delicate flavor that's slightly floral. Use lychee juice as part of the base for this ice.

- 1   cup lychee juice
- ⅓   cup sugar
- ⅛   teaspoon coarse sea salt
- 1   tablespoon dried lavender
- ½   teaspoon grated lemon rind (from 1 lemon)
- ½   cup fresh lemon juice (about 4 lemons)
- 2   tablespoons water
- ¼   peeled cucumber (about 4 ounces), cut into large chunks

1. Combine first 3 ingredients in a small saucepan. Bring to a boil. Stir in lavender. Remove from heat; cover and steep 30 minutes.

2. Pour lychee mixture through a sieve into a medium bowl. Discard solids. Stir in lemon rind and lemon juice. Place bowl in a large ice-filled bowl for 5 minutes or until cool, stirring occasionally.

3. Place 2 tablespoons water and cucumber in a blender; process until smooth. Stir into lychee mixture.

4. Pour mixture into an 8-inch square glass or ceramic baking dish. Cover and freeze until partially frozen (about 1 hour). Scrape with a fork, crushing any lumps. Freeze, scraping with a fork every 30 minutes, 1½ hours, or until completely frozen. Serves 5 (serving size: ½ cup)

CALORIES 84; FAT 0g (sat 0g, mono 0g, poly 0g); PROTEIN 0.2g; CARB 22.3g; FIBER 0.2g; CHOL 0mg; IRON 0mg; SODIUM 60mg; CALC 4mg

lemon granita

Be sure to use just the colored part of the citrus skin; the white part beneath, the pith, is bitter.

- 1   cup water
- ½   cup sugar
- 6   (2 x ½-inch) lemon rind strips
- 2   (2 x ½-inch) orange rind strips
- ¾   cup fresh lemon juice (about 8 lemons)
- ¼   cup fresh orange juice (about 1 orange)

1. Combine 1 cup water and sugar in a small saucepan. Bring to a boil over medium-high heat; reduce heat, and simmer 3 minutes, stirring until sugar dissolves. Remove from heat; stir in lemon and orange rind strips. Transfer rind mixture to a bowl; cool 10 minutes. Cover and refrigerate 30 minutes or until thoroughly chilled. Remove and discard lemon and orange rind strips. Stir in juices.

2. Pour into an 8-inch square glass or ceramic baking dish. Freeze until partially frozen (about 1 hour). Scrape with a fork, crushing any lumps. Freeze, scraping with a fork every 45 minutes, 3 hours or until completely frozen. Spoon mixture into chilled glasses or bowls. Serves 6 (serving size: about ½ cup)

CALORIES 78; FAT 0g (sat 0g, mono 0g, poly 0g); PROTEIN 0.2g; CARB 20.8g; FIBER 0.3g; CHOL 0mg; IRON 0mg; SODIUM 0mg; CALC 5mg

lime-coconut granita

Leave the base mix in the freezer overnight, and then scrape with a fork to get a pleasantly chunky texture. Garnish with additional grated lime rind, if desired.

2½ cups water

¾ cup sugar

1 tablespoon grated lime rind (from 2 limes)

½ cup fresh lime juice (about 7 limes)

½ cup light coconut milk

1. Combine all ingredients in a large saucepan over medium heat. Cook 3 minutes or until sugar dissolves, stirring constantly. Remove from heat, and cool completely.

2. Pour mixture into an 11 x 7–inch glass or ceramic baking dish. Cover and freeze 8 hours or until firm. Remove mixture from freezer; let stand 10 minutes. Scrape entire mixture with a fork until fluffy. Serves 8 (serving size: ½ cup)

CALORIES 85; FAT 0.8g (sat 0.7g, mono 0g, poly 0g); PROTEIN 0.3g; CARB 20.7g; FIBER 0.1g; CHOL 0mg; IRON 0mg; SODIUM 6mg; CALC 5mg

mexican chocolate ice

This frozen version of Mexican hot chocolate won high praise from tasters. It has a subtle cinnamon flavor and gets a kick from ground red pepper. Use non-dairy chocolate syrup to make this completely dairy-free.

2 **cups chocolate light soy milk**

⅓ **cup chocolate syrup**

½ **teaspoon vanilla extract**

⅜ **teaspoon ground cinnamon**

⅛ **teaspoon ground red pepper**

Chocolate curls (optional)

Cinnamon sticks (optional)

1. Combine all ingredients in the freezer can of an ice-cream freezer; freeze according to manufacturer's instructions. Spoon ice into a freezer-safe container; cover and freeze 2 hours or until firm. Scoop into dessert dishes, and garnish with chocolate curls and cinnamon sticks, if desired. Serves 5 (serving size: ½ cup)

CALORIES 103; FAT 0.6g (sat 0g, mono 0.2g, poly 0.4g); PROTEIN 2.6g; CARB 21.8g; FIBER 0.9g; CHOL 0mg; IRON 1mg; SODIUM 53mg; CALC 122mg

papaya guava granita

The tropical nectars make this an intensely flavored granita—and there's a nutrition bonus, too: Both papaya and guava give you a dose of vitamins A and C.

1   cup guava nectar

1   cup papaya nectar

⅓   cup sugar

½   teaspoon grated orange rind (from 1 orange)

¼   cup fresh orange juice (about 1 orange)

1. Combine first 3 ingredients a medium saucepan. Cook, stirring constantly, over medium heat 3 minutes or just until sugar dissolves. Place pan in a large ice-filled bowl; cool completely, stirring occasionally.

2. Stir in orange rind and juice. Pour mixture into a 13 x 9–inch glass or ceramic baking dish. Freeze until partially frozen (about 2 hours). Scrape with a fork, crushing any lumps. Freeze, scraping with a fork every hour, 2 hours or until completely frozen. Spoon into dessert dishes. Serves 8 (serving size: ½ cup)

CALORIES 73; FAT 0.1g (sat 0g, mono 0g, poly 0g); PROTEIN 0.2g; CARB 18.5g; FIBER 0.5g; CHOL 0mg; IRON 0mg; SODIUM 3mg; CALC 6mg

peach limeade granita

If you prefer to serve this as a beverage, skip the freezing and scraping steps and serve the limeade over ice.

4   cups water

1⅓ cups sugar

3   cups unpeeled peach slices (about 1 pound whole peaches)

6   mint leaves

1⅓ cups fresh lime juice (about 12 limes)

Peach slices (optional)

Mint sprigs (optional)

1. Combine 4 cups water and next 3 ingredients (through mint leaves) in a medium saucepan. Bring to a boil; reduce heat, and simmer, uncovered, 5 minutes. Cool 40 minutes. Remove and discard mint.

2. Place half of peach mixture in a blender; process until smooth. Pour pureed peach mixture into a 13 x 9-inch glass or ceramic baking dish. Combine remaining peach mixture and lime juice in blender; process until smooth. Add to baking dish.

3. Freeze until partially frozen (about 2 hours). Scrape with a fork, crushing any lumps. Freeze, scraping with a fork every 45 minutes, 1½ hours or until completely frozen. Scoop into dessert dishes, and garnish with peach slices and mint sprigs, if desired. Serves 8 (serving size: about 1 cup)

CALORIES 162; FAT 0.2g (sat 0g, mono 0g, poly 0.1g); PROTEIN 0.7g; CARB 42.4g; FIBER 1g; CHOL 0mg; IRON 0.2mg; SODIUM 1mg; CALC 10mg

peach-basil ice

Our Test Kitchen used fresh, ripe summer peaches in this ice; however, substitute frozen peaches in a pinch.

⅔ **cup sugar**

10 **to 12 medium basil leaves**

4 **cups fresh peach slices (about 1½ pounds whole peaches)**

⅔ **cup water**

⅓ **cup fresh lemon juice (about 3 lemons)**

1. Place sugar in a blender; process until very finely ground. Add basil; process until finely minced. Pour into an 8-inch square glass or ceramic baking dish.

2. Combine peach slices, ⅔ cup water, and lemon juice in blender; process until smooth. Pour juice mixture over sugar mixture, and stir until sugar dissolves. Cover and freeze until partially frozen (about 1 hour). Scrape with a fork, crushing any lumps. Freeze, scraping with a fork every hour, 4 hours or until completely frozen and fluffy. Serves 7 (serving size: ½ cup)

CALORIES 112; FAT 0.2g (sat 0g, mono 0.1g, poly 0.1g); PROTEIN 0.9g; CARB 28.6g; FIBER 1.3g; CHOL 0mg; IRON 0.3mg; SODIUM 0mg; CALC 8mg

pineapple-coconut ice

3 cups (1-inch) cubed fresh
 pineapple

1 (13.6-ounce) can light
 coconut milk

⅓ cup sugar

½ teaspoon grated lime rind
 (from 1 lime)

2 tablespoons fresh lime juice
 (about 2 limes)

7 teaspoons flaked sweetened
 coconut, toasted (optional)

1. Place first 5 ingredients in a blender; process until smooth. Pour into an 8-inch square glass or ceramic baking dish. Cover and freeze until partially frozen (about 2 hours). Scrape with a fork, crushing any lumps. Freeze 1 hour or until completely frozen; scrape entire mixture with a fork until fluffy. Divide ice among 7 dishes, and top each serving with 1 teaspoon coconut, if desired. Serves 7 (serving size: 1 cup)

CALORIES 82; FAT 0.9g (sat 0.7g, mono 0g, poly 0g); PROTEIN 0.6g; CARB 19.6g; FIBER 1g; CHOL 0mg; IRON 0.2mg; SODIUM 3mg; CALC 10mg

pink grapefruit sorbet

In this two-ingredient refreshing palate cleanser, the sugar tames the tartness of grapefruit juice. A serving delivers about two-thirds of your RDA for vitamin C, and only 145 calories.

3 cups fresh pink grapefruit juice (about 4 grapefruits), divided **¾ cup sugar**

1. Combine ½ cup grapefruit juice and sugar in a small saucepan over medium heat. Cook until sugar dissolves, stirring frequently.

2. Combine sugar mixture and 2½ cups grapefruit juice in a medium bowl; cover and refrigerate until chilled.

3. Pour mixture into the freezer can of an ice-cream freezer; freeze according to manufacturer's instructions. Spoon sorbet into a freezer-safe container; cover and freeze 1 hour or until firm. Serves 6 (serving size: ⅔ cup)

CALORIES 146; FAT 0.1g (sat 0g, mono 0g, poly 0g); PROTEIN 0.6g; CARB 36.6g; FIBER 0g; CHOL 0mg; IRON 0.3mg; SODIUM 1mg; CALC 11mg

raspberry-lemon ice

For a flavor variation, substitute lime juice and lime rind for the lemon. Garnish with fresh raspberries and a lemon slice on a skewer, or with a twist of lemon rind, if desired.

6 **cups fresh raspberries**

¾ **cup sugar**

1 **teaspoon grated lemon rind (from 1 lemon)**

3 **tablespoons fresh lemon juice (about 2 lemons)**

2 **tablespoons coarsely chopped fresh mint leaves**

1. Place all ingredients in a blender; process until smooth. Pour mixture through a sieve into an 8-inch square glass or ceramic baking dish. Cover and freeze until partially frozen (about 1 hour). Scrape with a fork, crushing any lumps. Freeze, scraping with a fork every hour, 4 hours or until completely frozen. Serves 10 (serving size: ½ cup)

CALORIES 98; FAT 0.5g (sat 0g, mono 0.1g, poly 0.3g); PROTEIN 0.9g; CARB 24.4g; FIBER 4.9g; CHOL 0mg; IRON 0.5mg; SODIUM 1mg; CALC 20mg

rhubarb, strawberry, and thyme granita

Thyme sprigs are steeped with the rhubarb in this herb-infused fruit granita, but an additional 1 teaspoon of finely chopped fresh thyme can be stirred into the rhubarb-strawberry mixture prior to freezing. Frozen rhubarb and strawberries may be substituted for fresh in this recipe.

¾ cup water

¾ cup sugar

2 cups chopped fresh rhubarb

3 thyme sprigs

2 cups sliced strawberries

2 tablespoons fresh lemon juice (about 2 lemons)

1. Combine ¾ cup water and sugar in a medium saucepan. Bring to a boil, stirring until sugar dissolves. Stir in rhubarb and thyme; return to a boil. Cover, reduce heat, and simmer 8 minutes or until rhubarb is tender. Place pan in a large ice-filled bowl for 10 minutes or until cool, stirring occasionally. Discard thyme sprigs.

2. Place rhubarb mixture, strawberries, and lemon juice in a blender; process until smooth. Pour mixture into an 8-inch square glass or ceramic baking dish. Cover and freeze until partially frozen (about 1 hour). Scrape with a fork, crushing any lumps. Freeze, scraping with a fork every hour, 4 hours or until completely frozen. Serves 10 (serving size: ½ cup)

CALORIES 75; FAT 0.2g (sat 0g, mono 0g, poly 0.1g); PROTEIN 0.5g; CARB 19.1g; FIBER 1.1g; CHOL 0mg; IRON 0.2mg; SODIUM 1mg; CALC 27mg

salted honeydew-grape granita

This pretty lime-green granita pairs honeydew melon with green grapes for a cooling treat. The hit of sea salt boosts flavor.

½   cup water

½   cup sugar

2   cups (2-inch) cubed honeydew melon

2   cups seedless green grapes

3   tablespoons fresh lime juice (about 2 large limes)

⅛   teaspoon coarse sea salt

1. Combine ½ cup water and sugar in a small saucepan. Bring to a boil, stirring until sugar dissolves. Place pan in a large ice-filled bowl for 25 minutes or until cool, stirring occasionally.

2. Place sugar syrup, melon, and remaining ingredients in a blender; process until smooth. Pour mixture into an 8-inch square glass or ceramic baking dish. Cover and freeze until partially frozen (about 1 hour). Scrape with a fork, crushing any lumps. Freeze, scraping with a fork every hour, 3 hours or until completely frozen. Serves 16 (serving size: ½ cup)

CALORIES 46; FAT 0.1g (sat 0g, mono 0g, poly 0g); PROTEIN 0.3g; CARB 11.9g; FIBER 0.4g; CHOL 0mg; IRON 0.1mg; SODIUM 22mg; CALC 4mg

southern sweet tea granita

A long steep draws out the deeper flavors of the tea; take care not to squeeze the tea bags to avoid making the granita bitter. Garnish the granita with lemon or mint sprigs, if desired.

3   **cups water**

3   **English breakfast or other black tea bags**

½   **cup sugar**

2   **tablespoons fresh lemon juice (about 2 lemons)**

2   **tablespoons honey**

1. Bring 3 cups water to a boil in a medium saucepan; remove from heat. Add tea bags; cover and steep 10 minutes.

2. Remove and discard tea bags. Add sugar, stirring until dissolved. Add lemon juice and honey, stirring until honey dissolves. Place pan in a large ice-filled bowl for 5 minutes or until cool, stirring occasionally.

3. Pour tea mixture into an 11 x 7-inch glass or ceramic baking dish. Cover and freeze until partially frozen (about 1 hour). Scrape with a fork, crushing any lumps. Freeze, scraping with a fork every 30 minutes, 1 hour or until completely frozen. Serves 8 (serving size: ½ cup)

CALORIES 66; FAT 0g (sat 0g, mono 0g, poly 0g); PROTEIN 0g; CARB 17.3g; FIBER 0g; CHOL 0mg; IRON 0mg; SODIUM 0mg; CALC 1mg

spicy mango granita

Garnish with additional red pepper for more kick, or with lime rind curls.

4   cups cubed peeled ripe mango

6   tablespoons sugar

¼   cup fresh orange juice (about 1 orange)

3   tablespoons fresh lime juice (about 2 large limes)

⅜   teaspoon ground red pepper

Dash of salt

1. Combine all ingredients in a small saucepan; bring to a boil. Reduce heat, and simmer 10 minutes. Remove from heat; let stand 10 minutes. Pour mixture into a blender; process until smooth. Strain mixture through a sieve over a bowl, and discard solids. Pour into an 11 x 7-inch glass or ceramic baking dish; cool. Cover and freeze 45 minutes; scrape with a fork. Freeze. Scrape every 45 minutes until completely frozen (about 6 hours total freezing time). Remove from freezer; scrape entire mixture with a fork until fluffy. Serves 6 (serving size: about ½ cup)

CALORIES 127; FAT 0.3g (sat 0.1g, mono 0.1g, poly 0.1g); PROTEIN 0.7g; CARB 33.1g; FIBER 2.1g; CHOL 0mg; IRON 0mg; SODIUM 2mg; CALC 13mg

strawberry granita

If you'd like to spruce up this granita, top with chopped or halved fresh strawberries and grated lemon zest.

½ **cup sugar**

½ **cup warm water**

3 **cups sliced strawberries**

2 **tablespoons fresh lemon juice (about 2 lemons)**

1. Combine sugar and ½ cup warm water in a blender; process until sugar dissolves. Add strawberries and juice; process until smooth.

2. Pour mixture into an 8-inch square glass or ceramic baking dish. Cover and freeze 3 hours; stir well. Cover and freeze 5 hours or overnight. Remove mixture from freezer; let stand at room temperature 10 minutes. Scrape entire mixture with a fork until fluffy. Serves 4 (serving size: 1 cup)

CALORIES 136; FAT 0.5g (sat 0g, mono 0.1g, poly 0.2g); PROTEIN 0.8g; CARB 34.4g; FIBER 2.9g; CHOL 0mg; IRON 0.5mg; SODIUM 2mg; CALC 18mg

tomato watermelon ice

Tomato and watermelon are a popular summer salad. Here, they complement each other in an ice. This is a great choice for an appetizer or a refresher between courses. Serve with small watermelon wedges, if desired.

2 cups chopped watermelon

1 cup chopped seeded tomato

¼ cup chopped seeded peeled cucumber

2 tablespoons sugar

2 tablespoons chopped red bell pepper

1 tablespoon fresh lime juice (about 1 lime)

1 tablespoon fresh cilantro leaves

1 teaspoon minced seeded jalapeño pepper

⅛ teaspoon celery salt

1. Place all ingredients in a blender; process until smooth.

2. Pour watermelon mixture into an 8-inch square glass or ceramic baking dish. Freeze 1 hour; stir. Freeze 2 hours or until completely frozen, scraping with a fork every hour. Serves 5 (serving size: 1 cup)

CALORIES 47; FAT 0.2g (sat 0g, mono 0g, poly 0.1g); PROTEIN 0.8g; CARB 11.4g; FIBER 0.8g; CHOL 0mg; IRON 1mg; SODIUM 28mg; CALC 11mg

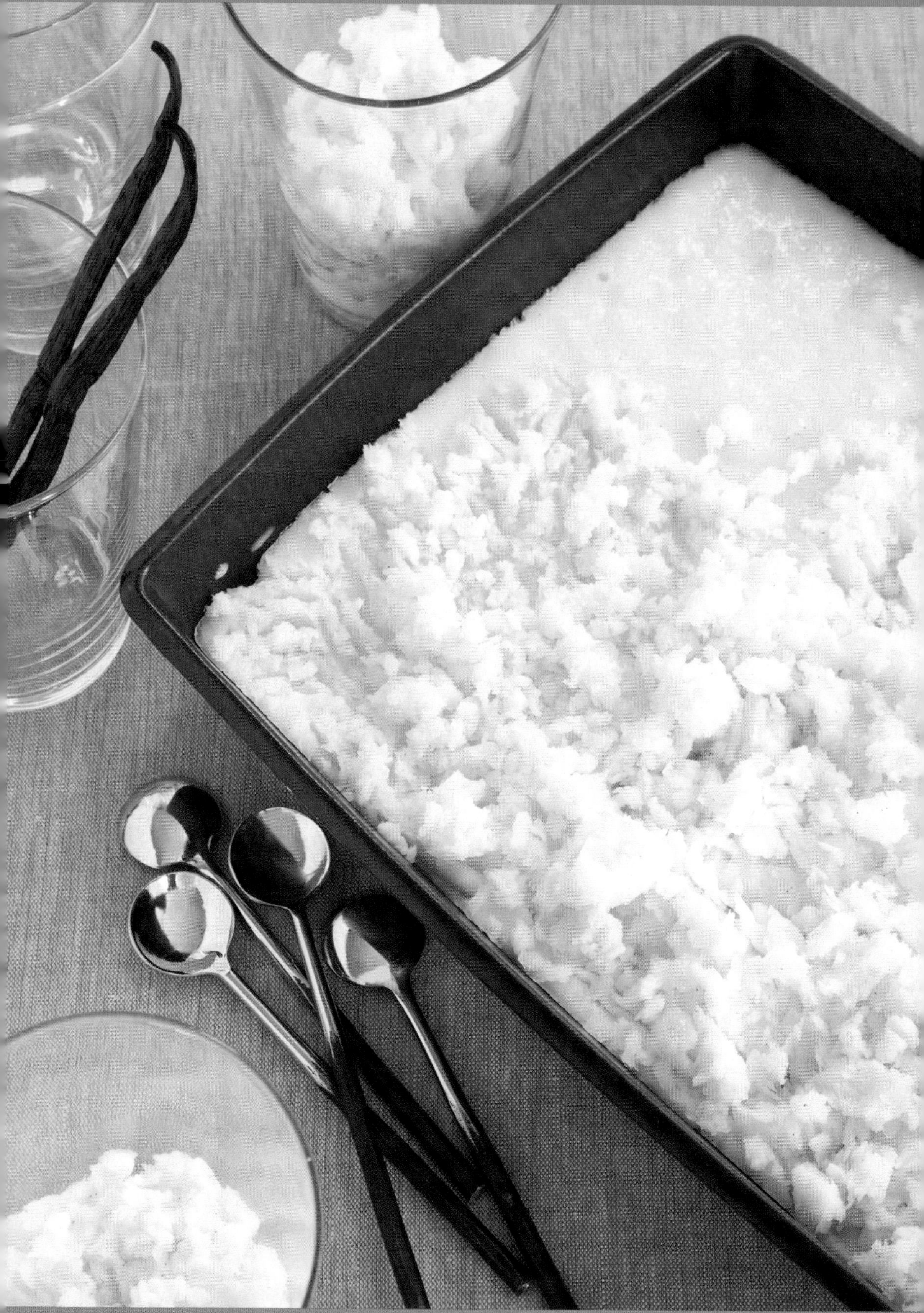

vanilla ice

This ice will remind you of making ice cream out of snow. While many commercial vanilla desserts are too cloying to let the vanilla flavor shine through, this three-ingredient recipe will show you that vanilla is anything but plain. You can use an equal amount of vanilla paste for the extract; it will create an ice flecked with vanilla seeds.

4 cups 2% reduced-fat milk

½ cup sugar

1 teaspoon vanilla extract

1. Combine all ingredients in a bowl, stirring with a whisk until sugar dissolves. Pour into an 8-inch square glass or ceramic baking dish. Cover and freeze until partially frozen (about 1 hour). Scrape with a fork, crushing any lumps. Freeze, scraping with a fork every hour, 2 hours or until completely frozen. Serves 7 (serving size: 1 cup)

CALORIES 127; FAT 2.8g (sat 1.8g, mono 0.8g, poly 0.1g); PROTEIN 4.6g; CARB 21g; FIBER 0g; CHOL 11.2mg; IRON 0mg; SODIUM 57mg; CALC 163mg

watermelon and lime granita

Make this in a spare moment on the weekend, then serve later in the week for a no-fuss dessert.

½ **cup sugar**

½ **cup water**

4 **cups cubed seedless watermelon**

½ **cup fresh lime juice (about 6 limes)**

Lime slices (optional)

1. Place sugar and ½ cup water in a small saucepan over medium-high heat; bring to a boil. Reduce heat and simmer 3 minutes. Remove from heat. Place sugar mixture in a small bowl; cool 10 minutes. Cover and chill at least 30 minutes.

2. Place sugar mixture, watermelon, and juice in a blender; process until smooth. Pour watermelon mixture into an 11 x 7–inch glass or ceramic baking dish; cover and freeze 3 hours. Stir well.

3. Cover and freeze at least 2 hours or overnight. Remove mixture from freezer, and let stand at room temperature 10 minutes. Scrape entire mixture with a fork until fluffy. Serve with lime slices, if desired. Serves 6 (serving size: ½ cup)

CALORIES 100; FAT 0.2g (sat 0g, mono 0g, poly 0.1g); PROTEIN 0.7g; CARB 26g; FIBER 0.5g; CHOL 0mg; IRON 0.3mg; SODIUM 2mg; CALC 11mg

Nutritional Analysis

How to Use It and Why

Glance at the end of any *Cooking Light* recipe, and you'll see how committed we are to helping you make the best of today's light cooking. With chefs, registered dietitians, home economists, and a computer system that analyzes every ingredient we use, *Cooking Light* gives you authoritative dietary detail like no other magazine. We go to such lengths so you can see how our recipes fit into your healthful eating plan. If you're trying to lose weight, the calorie and fat figures will probably help most. But if you're keeping a close eye on the sodium, cholesterol, and saturated fat in your diet, we provide those numbers, too. And because many women don't get enough iron or calcium, we can help there, as well. Finally, there's a fiber analysis for those of us who don't get enough roughage.

Here's a helpful guide to put our nutritional analysis numbers into perspective. Remember, one size doesn't fit all, so take your lifestyle, age, and circumstances into consideration when determining your nutrition needs. For example, pregnant or breast-feeding women need more protein, calories, and calcium. And women older than 50 need 1,200mg of calcium daily, 200mg more than the amount recommended for younger women.

In Our Nutritional Analysis, We Use These Abbreviations

sat	saturated fat	CARB	carbohydrates	CALC	calcium
mono	monounsaturated fat	CHOL	cholesterol	g	gram
poly	polyunsaturated fat			mg	milligram

Daily Nutrition Guide

	Women ages 25 to 50	Women over 50	Men ages 24 to 50	Men over 50
Calories	2,000	2,000 or less	2,700	2,500
Protein	50g	50g or less	63g	60g
Fat	65g or less	65g or less	88g or less	83g or less
Saturated Fat	20g or less	20g or less	27g or less	25g or less
Carbohydrates	304g	304g	410g	375g
Fiber	25g to 35g	25g to 35g	25g to 35g	25g to 35g
Cholesterol	300mg or less	300mg or less	300mg or less	300mg or less
Iron	18mg	8mg	8mg	8mg
Sodium	2,300mg or less	1,500mg or less	2,300mg or less	1,500mg or less
Calcium	1,000mg	1,200mg	1,000mg	1,000mg

The nutritional values used in our calculations either come from The Food Processor, Version 10.4 (ESHA Research), or are provided by food manufacturers.

Metric Equivalents

The information in the following charts is provided to help cooks outside the United States successfully use the recipes in this book. All equivalents are approximate.

Cooking/Oven Temperatures

	Fahrenheit	Celsius	Gas Mark
Freeze Water	32° F	0° C	
Room Temp.	68° F	20° C	
Boil Water	212° F	100° C	
Bake	325° F	160° C	3
	350° F	180° C	4
	375° F	190° C	5
	400° F	200° C	6
	425° F	220° C	7
	450° F	230° C	8
Broil			Grill

Liquid Ingredients by Volume

¼ tsp	=					1 ml
½ tsp	=					2 ml
1 tsp	=					5 ml
3 tsp	=	1 Tbsp =	½ fl oz	=		15 ml
2 Tbsp	=	⅛ cup =	1 fl oz	=		30 ml
4 Tbsp	=	¼ cup =	2 fl oz	=		60 ml
5⅓ Tbsp	=	⅓ cup =	3 fl oz	=		80 ml
8 Tbsp	=	½ cup =	4 fl oz	=		120 ml
10⅔ Tbsp	=	⅔ cup =	5 fl oz	=		160 ml
12 Tbsp	=	¾ cup =	6 fl oz	=		180 ml
16 Tbsp	=	1 cup =	8 fl oz	=		240 ml
1 pt	=	2 cups =	16 fl oz	=		480 ml
1 qt	=	4 cups =	32 fl oz	=		960 ml
			33 fl oz	=	1000 ml	= 1 l

Dry Ingredients by Weight

(To convert ounces to grams, multiply the number of ounces by 30.)

1 oz	=	¹⁄₁₆ lb	=	30 g
4 oz	=	¼ lb	=	120 g
8 oz	=	½ lb	=	240 g
12 oz	=	¾ lb	=	360 g
16 oz	=	1 lb	=	480 g

Length

(To convert inches to centimeters, multiply the number of inches by 2.5.)

1 in	=				2.5 cm	
6 in	=	½ ft		=	15 cm	
12 in	=	1 ft		=	30 cm	
36 in	=	3 ft	= 1 yd	=	90 cm	
40 in	=				100 cm	= 1 m

Equivalents for Different Types of Ingredients

Standard Cup	Fine Powder (ex. flour)	Grain (ex. rice)	Granular (ex. sugar)	Liquid Solids (ex. butter)	Liquid (ex. milk)
1	140 g	150 g	190 g	200 g	240 ml
¾	105 g	113 g	143 g	150 g	180 ml
⅔	93 g	100 g	125 g	133 g	160 ml
½	70 g	75 g	95 g	100 g	120 ml
⅓	47 g	50 g	63 g	67 g	80 ml
¼	35 g	38 g	48 g	50 g	60 ml
⅛	18 g	19 g	24 g	25 g	30 ml

Index